# WITBOY IN AFRICA

## Diary of a Troublemaker

## DEON MAAS

TAFELBERG

Tafelberg

an imprint of NB Publishers,

40 Heerengracht, Cape Town

© Deon Maas (2010)

Cover design by Louis Minnaar

Book design and typesetting by Jean van der Meulen

Translated by Lynette Posthumus

Edited by Lindsay Norman

Map on p 88 by John Hall

Photography by Deon Maas

Set in 11/14 Perpetua Std

Printed and bound by Interpak Books, Pietermaritzburg

First edition, first impression 2010

ISBN 978-0-624-04833-6

For Gerrad and Axl because I was never there
and for Veda because she was …
and lastly for my rock, Gerrit.

Just because I am white skinned
Dont make me european
You know I didnt sail here
I was born right in the Frere (thats Frere hospital baby)

I dont know Jan van Riebeeck
I dont believe in parliament
I didnt vote till '94
So stop breaking down my front door

**"Afreakan" by the Transkei Cowboys**

# CONTENTS

Foreword . . . . . . . . . . . . . . . . . . . . . . . . . . . . . . . . . . . . vii

**Two Africans in New York** . . . . . . . . . . . . . . . . . . . . **1**

**1  Guerillas in the mist** . . . . . . . . . . . . . . . . . . . . . . . . **3**

**2  Honeymooning in Africa** . . . . . . . . . . . . . . . . . . **37**

**3  The Five Nations tour** . . . . . . . . . . . . . . . . . . . **71**

**Map of Nigeria** . . . . . . . . . . . . . . . . . . . . . . . . . . **88**

**4  Nigeria 101** . . . . . . . . . . . . . . . . . . . . . . . . . . . **89**

**Witboy's travel tips** . . . . . . . . . . . . . . . . . . . . . **135**

**5  Reality TV: a Rude Awakening** . . . . . . . . . . . . . **139**

**6  Diary of the end of a marriage** . . . . . . . . . . . . **177**

Epilogue . . . . . . . . . . . . . . . . . . . . . . . . . . . . . . . **203**

Suggested reading . . . . . . . . . . . . . . . . . . . . . . . . . **207**

# FOREWORD

HAVE ALWAYS BEEN fascinated by the exotic places where many authors write their forewords. When it was my turn, I was sitting cross-legged on the floor of the departure hall of Murtalla Mohammed Airport in Lagos. There was a restaurant on either side of me.

To my left was an expensive restaurant with French bread and perfectly prepared cappuccinos (well, perfect for Nigeria). A European soccer match filled a big screen television but thankfully the sound was off. The people in the expensive restaurant sat alone at their tables, waiting for flights to countries like France, Scotland, Lebanon, the USA ...

In the cheap cafeteria with the plastic chairs on my right I heard more Afrikaans than I would have in a restaurant in Joburg. The cafeteria was mostly filled with white men, probably affirmative action victims forced to sell their services in other African countries. I gathered that most of them were on their first visit to Nigeria. Strangers to each other, they exchanged stories about their experiences. Afrikaans was the unifying factor. They were a motley crew: engineers, farmers, divers on oil rigs – and then there was me. I was there to make a television programme.

Everyone is always trying to help Africa, but most of the time they end up achieving the opposite. Take Madonna, for instance, who invaded Malawi like a modern day slave trader, picked out the prettiest little orphan and took him home. Or the carbon copy BBC correspondent who wrote a bestseller on how to fix up some or other African country that he'd lived in for a grand total of six months.

I don't try to emulate BBC correspondents in my book and I don't have any ground-breaking insights. After travelling for more than a decade on the continent, I've simply forgotten which of my stories I've shared with which of my friends. So I thought it might be a good idea to put all my experiences into one book.

But as I started writing, the book took on an extra dimension that made me think about identity and race. My travels have taught me that in Africa race is regarded as extremely important, irrespective of the country you're visiting, the level of education of the people you meet or their income. Could I as a white, Afrikaans-speaking person really call myself an African? At the same time, I read esteemed author Elsa Joubert's *Die Staf van Monomotapa* (1964), which tells of her search for a mythical kingdom in Mozambique. The theme running through the book is her experiences as a white person in Africa. I realised that I wasn't the first person to wrestle with these questions.

There was another reason why I wrote the book. Firstly, completely out of the blue I got an offer from Kerneels Breytenbach, then head of publications at NB Publishers, to put my experiences in writing. Like most good Calvinists (in my case, lapsed Calvinist) I have a great deal of respect for older men with beards, so I had to agree. Secondly, I got a publisher by the name of Annie Olivier who understands what I'm trying to say and does not try to change my language or style. In the eighties when I was still a journalist, there were many unpleasant moments between me and the elderly gentleman at *Rooi Rose* who had to subedit my copy. And the blockhead at *Huisgenoot* who got hold of my work wisely refrained from giving me his home address, foiling my plans for a late night visit.

I firmly believe that you'll never understand a country's psyche unless you know something of its history. Before I go on a trip I spend hours on the internet and in bookshops collecting information. It gives me a better idea of what to expect and it impresses the local people no end that you took some trouble to learn more about their country.

I started reading books even before I went to school and when I was fourteen my dad bought me an old second-hand typewriter from the Old Mutual. (Many rejection slips followed that gift, but let's not go into that right now.) My parents never invested in a holiday home and so we went on a new adventure every school holiday. Before we left I would read about the places we were going to visit, especially the history, and then I'd force my dad to stop at every single national monument or historical site along the way.

There's a kind of traveller who leaves at five o'clock in the morning and only stops twice before he reaches his destination. The first time is to fill up and the second time is to give his noisy and troublesome kids who won't stop complaining a good hiding. I don't fall into this category, but my father definitely does. As a child I was often left by the side of the road because I was such a demanding child. I'm still a rather demanding person, but now at least I have my own car and I can even smoke while I'm driving. Sometimes it's pretty good fun to be grown-up.

And today my father has to stop at every second farm stall, because my mother wants to buy gifts for the friends they will be staying with. My dad simply had to accept his fate even though if it was up to him he would have left at o5:oo am and only stopped twice during the trip.

Although I still read up on places before I travel, things have changed dramatically since I discovered an alternative source of knowledge about distant cities, namely its nightlife, along with beer and girls who like guys with foreign accents. Now when I'm travelling to foreign cities my favourite places are bars, clubs and coffee shops. I do the necessary research, but often only use it to impress people – like girls who like foreign accents. I use my local contacts as tour guides, and also get them to show me the city's underbelly. Large parts of this book were therefore written on the back of till slips in bars. If there are any factual errors I apologise in advance. Blame the liquor.

So this book is not a travel guide crammed with suggestions of which museums, old buildings or nature reserves you have to visit. They do feature, but somewhere in the background. This book doesn't even cover an eighth of all African countries, but focuses on some of the places that have made an indelible impression on me. It doesn't try to explore the entire continent like Bill Bryson's books – that seems like way too much work.

I don't travel with a kangaroo pouch and a plan. Most of my adventures happen accidentally. "Fools rush in where angels fear to tread" was probably coined with me in mind. The fact that I'm still here is solid proof that someone is watching out for me. The greater power that planned my life has a good sense of humour. He (or She) instilled a keen sense of adventure and a burning desire to explore foreign parts in a cowboy-like manner.

This means that I'm just as comfortable in Antwerp as in Kigali, or between the billboards on 42$^{nd}$ Avenue in New York and heavily armed soldiers at a roadblock in the east of the Congo. This also means that I can keep my cool while I have to negotiate with a soldier in Ray-Ban Aviators who is high on coke and waving a loaded AK47 in the air.

About 90% of this book is the truth, but the remaining 10% is total hogwash. One should not believe everything one reads and by not saying which 90% is the truth, I hope to keep a few attorneys off my case. No one's ego or reputation was damaged during the writing of this book, but quite a few names were changed to protect them (and me). Luckily the events on which my stories are based all happened outside South African borders, so I hope the long arm of the law won't be able to reach me.

I would like to ask my parents' forgiveness in advance since I am bound to embarrass them yet again. I know that many of the things

I say and do make them wonder where they failed in my education. I can only say it's entirely their fault. In an era known for narrow-minded thinking they encouraged me to investigate all things and have opinions about important issues. They made me who I am today and for that I'm eternally indebted to them.

For the record, I wish to state that I was well brought up, but I was seduced by the evils of sex, alcohol, drugs, pop music and a wild imagination. And about that I have no regrets.

To my children: please do as I say and not as I do. I realise that it must be tough to have a dad who is an eternal teenager and that you got all kinds of handmade wooden toys as gifts when you really wanted Nintendo.

Then I would like to thank Pauli who let me to spend so much time on something that makes so little money and that put our business, Meerkat Media, under pressure. She had to keep the household running while I gallivanted all over the world. She was the one who had to cope with children in police cells, water and electricity accounts and home renovations while I collected information like some hunter gatherer. Pauli also allowed me to recount some stories that other women might not have been comfortable with.

They say every story has a beginning, a middle and an end. Strange that one never knows who "they" are. It could be the same "they" who heard that the policeman's wife visited the mechanic while hubby was out of town too long. In that case "they" would be right. Every story has to have a beginning, but I'm not exactly sure where the middle of this story is. Between my publisher and the editor I'm sure they'll sort it out. A story's ending is not necessarily determined by the author. If he's lucky, he'll keep the reader's attention up to the last page. If not, it will end up on the shelf of a second-hand bookshop or it will become one of those last minute birthday gifts.

Hopefully I'll succeed in tearing you away from your television set for a few minutes. Television is bad for your sex life and reproduces life in short sound bites without getting to the crux of the matter. Not that I necessarily always get to the point, but the adventure on the way there is far more important than anything else.

In conclusion, a message to all the airlines I have used through the years: It sucks to fly in economy class and your client service is horrible. How do you expect me to follow a movie's dialogue with cheap earphones made in China, while everyone around me is wide awake and chattering away, just because you wouldn't ply them with enough alcohol? You should also seriously consider giving all children under the age of ten a Valium before allowing them on the plane. Onboard frustration is the real danger, not nail clippers and cigarette lighters.

When I'm president one day, I'm going to lock you all up.

Deon Maas*
Murtalla Mohammed Airport
Lagos, Nigeria

---

\*     Deon Maas is Witboy, but Witboy isn't Deon Maas.

# TWO AFRICANS IN NEW YORK

## Harlem, 2002

Politically correct African American journalist (Journalist): "How do you see the future of African Americans?"

Famous black South African performer (Performer): "What is an African American?"

Journalist: "You know, black Americans?"

Performer: "Why do you call them 'Africans'?"

Journalist: "Because that's where they're from."

Performer: "You mean blacks here call themselves 'African'?"

Journalist: "Yes, didn't you know?"

Performer: "My white friend here is African. Black Americans are not."

Journalist: "Why do you say that?"

Performer: "You can only call yourself African if you can shit behind a bush and wipe your arse with leaves."

Journalist: "I can't write that."

Performer: "Well, then I guess that's the end of the interview. Hey Deon, wanna go and irritate some more niggers?"

1

# GUERILLAS IN THE MIST
Rwanda, 1998

I WAS STANDING IN the international terminal at the Johannesburg airport surrounded by a mountain of sound equipment. Its joint capacity could deafen a whole stadium of people for days. Despite the air-conditioning the guys carrying the equipment were sweating.

I was also sweating, but it wasn't to do with physical exhaustion. This was my first trip into Darkest Africa. A product of white suburbia, I had been warned against "die Swart Gevaar" my entire life. Now I was walking into the lion's den, much like Daniel. The only difference was that it was not my religious conviction that nudged me into the lion's den, but a warped sense of adventure. I was doing it entirely voluntarily.

While the guys were still bringing in more stuff, it was my job to charm the cute young lady behind the counter, because we were in for an excess baggage fine. I had R10 000 cash in my pocket to sort out any problems, but as our whole trip lay ahead I had to keep the excess as low as possible.

The sticky, sweaty feeling I was experiencing wasn't only due to my uncertainty about my first visit north of the Limpopo. The welfare of more than a dozen people weighed heavily on me. Well, actually not people, musicians. Musicians are a special subspecies. They lose passports, miss flights, get drunk and end up in people's beds without knowing where the beds are. The cash might not last long.

It all started a few weeks ago. When my bosses at Gallo asked who would be interested in managing Lucky Dube's Rwandan tour I was the one who waved my arm in the air frantically like a teacher's pet. It was four years since the genocide in Rwanda and we had been a Rainbow Nation for four years. At that time Africa was still a fairly dark place for the average South African – especially if you were white.

Well, I thought, at least no one would confuse me with a Hutu or a Tutsi if anything did go wrong.

None of my black colleagues even considered going. The entire week before I left everyone at the office was extremely friendly to me. I had the distinct impression they thought they might not see me again. And the evening before our departure they even threw me a farewell bash.

My mother was terribly upset. The "but what are you going to do there, my child?" and the "why would you even consider going there?" questions were never ending. I never told her that I volunteered to go.

It's difficult travelling in Africa when your skin is white. The chances are slim that you'll be taken for a local and even if you are one, you'll still stand out. This means you'll be the constant target of beggars, curio salesmen, or anyone who sees you as a possible source of income. The reasoning is very basic: you are white, therefore you have money.

If you visit a bar on your own, your cell phone will inevitably be admired within minutes. Weird, but this is a favourite pick-up line in places like this. Numerous women (or rather girls) will sleep with you in exchange for a few dollars, an airline ticket out of the country or sometimes just for the chance to be seen with you.

I'm not into that kind of thing, but I'm the exception. One of the worst images in Africa is of a fat, perspiring Scot, Swede or other sinner with a pathetic hairstyle accompanied by three beautiful, clever back women who hang on to his every word. You just know he'd never get so lucky back home. And while he gets sloshed, the girls work up courage for the bedroom escapades. This happens everywhere and far too often.

Travelling becomes even more daunting when you are white, and just an ordinary tourist. Then you become the target for every single person sporting a uniform – the tweedledees and tweedledums of the bureaucracy. The expectation is that you will make some kind of donation towards their salary, funeral policy or their children's school fund. Sometimes Mr Uniform is thirsty and only wants a Coke or a cigarette. But you *will* fork out something. Paying up is the name of the African travelling game.

When you're travelling with someone like Lucky Dube, a total superstar in Africa, things change pretty quickly. You hang out with ministers. Your bodyguard is usually a senior security policeman – the kind you avoid like the plague when you're an ordinary tourist. And best of all, you get a safe pass letter, signed by someone high up in the hierarchy, which guarantees your safety in any tricky situation. You are actually hanging out with the baddies, but what the heck, if it makes you safe, so be it.

In Africa (as in most of the world) people are only nice until they get power or money. Then they turn into power crazed megalomaniacs whose only mission in life is to get more power and money. In this elite group everyone takes good care of each other, presidents included, because they are all in the same boat: If someone rocks the boat they'll all have to swim for their lives.

Rwanda is no exception and I wouldn't be surprised if this was the case when the Belgians were in power. When people say Africa is not for sissies, they really mean Rwanda. This place is hardcore. Don't be seduced by all the greenery – it harbours a vicious cruelty that is imbedded in the country's psyche.

At the time of the last genocide most Rwandans poured scorn on political correctness. Muslims were called "penguins" to their face.

Hutus knew they were "ugly and stupid", and only good for looking after cattle because that's what they had been told for centuries. If you don't believe me, read the newspapers of that time. You'll find it there in black and white, and we all know newspapers don't lie...

Thanks to the Belgians, ethnic division is now part of the country's genetics. Every coloniser in Africa was guilty of human rights violations and theft of precious resources. The Belgians, however, deserve special mention for cruelty and exploitation. Belgium never even officially colonised the Congo. In 1885 King Leopold simply claimed the country as his private property where he could do as he pleased. The state financed the infrastructure and the king pocketed the profits.

King Leopold's exploits in the Congo are infamous. His philosophy was to scare people into working harder to increase his own wealth. At that time rubber was an expensive and sought-after product in Europe and in the process of extracting it in the forests of the Congo King Leopold's henchmen murdered more than 10 million Congolese. People's head and hands were cut off and the heads displayed on poles as a barbaric warning – all in the name of rubber.

During King Leopold's reign of terror in the Congo, neighbouring Rwanda was under Belgian control. The country had very few natural resources and this was before the days when the wild gorillas attracted international tourists. Even though the Belgian government couldn't make the same kind of money from Rwanda that King Leopold made out of the Congo, they certainly used his tried and tested methods to increase production. Their technique to motivate workers was to give them eight lashes with a cane before work.

But the Belgian's special legacy to the Rwandese was ethnic hatred. The area's original inhabitants were the Twa pygmies who were not and to this day are not regarded as people by many Rwandese. In some remote parts of the country it was quite acceptable to serve them up for dinner. At least that's what was alleged in a newspaper. Today they form only 1% of the total population.

The first time I mentioned the Twa in Rwandese company the conversation stopped immediately and everybody burst out laughing. Why a mzungu would be interested in these baboons boggled their minds. I once saw a Twa man in a Rwandan village, but children beat him with sticks because he had the audacity to show his face in town. He was trying to get to the local clinic.

The Hutus and the Tutsis are the two largest ethnic groups in Rwanda. The Hutus look like Idi Amin and represent 84% of the population. The Tutsis represent 15% of the population and look like models. They are tall and thin with narrow noses and a light skin. The Belgians decided that the Tutsis were clever and the Hutus stupid. In their infinite wisdom they introduced a dompas system with which to indicate every person's ethnicity.

And to make absolutely sure that the two groups would never live in peace again, they decided that only the Tutsis could own land, and that the Hutus had to work for them. To top it off, a law was passed that only allowed Tutsis to receive any form of education. Not only were the Hutus stupid and ugly, but were now rendered illiterate. Their laws have a certain resonance with the ideologies of apartheid South Africa.

The Hutus were understandably more than a little peeved with the situation and in 1959 the first genocide took place. There were 100 000 deaths. The Tutsi king and about 200 000 of his followers had to flee the country and most of them ended up in Uganda. Among them was Paul Kagame, the current president of Rwanda.

When the Belgians decided to leave in 1962 they had to decide who would be granted power. The Tutsis were educated and had started to think independently. The Belgians did not think this was a good idea and so put the Hutus in power. In this way, the elderly white men of Europe argued, they could still control Rwanda from a distance. Suddenly the cow herders were in a position of power and the festering conflict, which was suppressed for centuries, erupted with unprecedented hatred.

In the late 1950s and early 1960s it was legal for a Hutu to murder a Tutsi with no consequences for the murderer. Tutsis were called *inyenzi's* (cockroaches).

In 1963 there was another genocide and thousands of Tutsis were murdered. As the victims were black and there was no international media to carry the news to the outside world, no one actually counted the bodies. However, it has since been described as the biggest genocide since the Holocaust.

By 1974 the Hutus were resenting the fact that there were still so many Tutsis in professional positions, especially in medicine, academics and education. They were all forced to resign … and again there was a massacre.

This was the country to which we were heading to stage a pop concert – a country suffering from permanent post traumatic stress syndrome, not fully recovered from its nightmares of four years ago.

Music is cunningly used by many a despot to calm the masses. It wasn't Lucky's first invitation to a country with extraordinary problems. His passport also bore the stamps of Sierra Leone and Liberia.

The airport in Kigali, with the imaginative name of Kigali International Airport, must have been designed in the seventies by a depressed architect. We arrived at a drab building with two entrances, one marked Arrivée/Arrival and the other VIP Arrivée/Arrival. There was little or no control over people's movements. The tarmac was like the local athletics track where eager television teams and radio and newspaper journalists dodged aircraft wings and jockeyed for first place to record the arrival of Africa's biggest superstar. Kigali International Airport is clearly not frequented by loads of celebs.

Lucky entered the airport via the VIP Arrivée, while the rest of us mere mortals used the Arrivée entrance. In a country where one's social status is the be all and end all, the news that you're nobody is not conveyed very subtly. There was only one important person on this occasion and even the men in black wearing black sunglasses to patrol the interior of the airport hardly gave our impressive Rwandan visas with their gorilla holograms a second glance.

The weather was surprisingly mild and the airport almost empty. The dejected immigration and customs officials soon realised this was not a day to cash in. Any false move made by them would mean the end of the concert. This was clearly set out in the contract with the promoter and it was his duty to see to it that everything went smoothly – otherwise his investment would fly back without laying the proverbial golden egg. Lucky had also insisted that the concert fee be deposited into his bank account before he packed his suitcases. It was a question of once bitten, twice shy ...

Kigali has 851 024 residents. On the way from the airport to the Windsor Umubano Hotel we saw 851 023 of them. As part of the marketing for the concert the promoter, Mister Vincent de Gaulle (don't forget the all important "Mister"), decided to take us on a short trip. We drove through the whole of Kigali while thousands of people, sometimes up to a hundred deep in places, lined the sides of the road to cheer Lucky. He rode in splendid isolation in a massive 4x4 – not unlike the pope, minus the bullet-proof glass. The crowds threw branches in front of his vehicle and went seriously ballistic.

The rest of the group, all twelve of us, travelled in a ten-seater bus called a matatu. The 4x4 kicked up a lot of dust and we had to follow shortly behind it as people were stepping onto the road to get a better look at Lucky who was standing up, waving from the open sunroof.

The matatu carrying us was a Japanese import since in Japan all vehicles have to be written off after five years in service. An entire economy has been built throughout Africa around these imports.

Once, a long, long time ago, the bus might have been five years old in Japan, but its African vacation had been going on for several years. The bus still carried Japanese lettering on its sides. No effort had been made to Rwandanise it and even the Rwandan number plate was rather scruffily hooked over the original Japanese one.

Sitting squashed between the window and one of Lucky's massively proportioned background singers, I wondered how much more I'd have to sacrifice for other people's happiness on this trip. Staring out at the sea of faces outside I noticed that the citizens of Kigali were clothed in tatters. The signs of urban poverty were all around me: dilapidated houses with clay walls and rusted corrugated iron roofs, thin dogs and children with swollen bellies. It was fascinating to see how Lucky brought happy smiles to their gaunt faces, and how their expressions changed to sheer amazement the moment they saw my white face squashed against the window. Hippies and missionaries travelled in the back of a bus, not your average whitey.

But at long last I was where I wanted to be. Smack-dab in the middle of Africa, busy fulfilling a childhood dream of adventure. Viva Mandela, viva!

For the next week I answered every incoming call on my cell with: "I'm in Rwanda right now, can this wait until I come back?" I enjoyed every moment of saying that sentence over and over again and people's reactions even more. I was a fearless adventurer and an intrepid pioneer. I was seeing and experiencing things that my friends, acquaintances and colleagues could only dream about. I finally realised what I wanted out of life – to travel as far and wide as possible.

This was before I knew the history of the hotel where we stayed. The Windsor Umubano Hotel, complete with an ornate crown on the W, was audacious enough to call itself "Kigali's resort within the city". This simply meant that there was a swimming pool. The hotel was situated on one of the many hills on which Kigali is built and surrounded by. All the important people lived on the hills of Kigali. This included the state buildings. The views are of the abject poverty in the valleys below. This conveyed the essence of the country's psyche.

When I entered the hotel, I had a vision of what it must have looked like thirty years ago. Men in suits and ladies in glittering gowns attending a ball while waiters serving delicacies prepared by French chefs moved unobtrusively between groups of guests. In the background local musicians played live music, and captains of industry had muted business discussions. But I was greeted by piped pan flute music in a hotel that tried its damndest, but could not even serve a decent hamburger.

The archaic accounting system of the restaurant meant that every beer had to be registered by two elderly gents in bowties who sat behind a wooden table in a corner. They issued a completed form written out in neat calligraphy-like handwriting on a hotel letter-head. The waiter then took the form to the barman who issued the beer and signed the form. But before the beer could be brought to you the signed form first had to be delivered back to the two bean counters – dare I call them beer counters? The beer was never cold and at the end of the evening you had to wait for half an hour for your account because everything had to be added up, signed off by the manager and finally handed to you.

In the hotel a Primus, one of the excellent local beers, cost R20. On the sidewalk in front of the hotel it went for R2. On top of that you were offered a wooden chair from where you could listen to local music and watch the afternoon traffic go by. Needless to say, the sidewalk became my favourite spot. Of course the more beers I polished, the more blurred the passing traffic became. I enjoyed hanging out with the local guys and we tried to exchange stories in broken English while the hotel's security guard stood as close to me as possible but without leaving the safe enclosure of the hotel. English may be the third most popular language in Rwanda following Kinyarwanda and French, but it is a very slow third.

On several occasions the guard warned me against the "bad people" I was hanging out with. It took me a while to realise he was referring to the Hutus. Physically I could not see a difference between him and the "bad people". The words "bad people", I soon realised, was the full extent of his command of the Queen's English. When I entered the hotel just after nightfall, I had to thump Kigali's dust out of my clothes while the guard who followed me shook his head and muttered under his breath. I was sure he complained bitterly to his wife every night. The mad mzungu who hung out with the "bad people" will surely feature in his memoirs.

In theory there was nothing wrong with the hotel. The lift was in working order, the toilets flushed and we even had hot water. But even as a fancy hotel in Africa it was still an anomaly. It was extremely clean and everyone knew their place. But the clinical aura bothered me and it was only when I found out more about the hotel's history that I understood why.

The thing is, the Windsor Umubano Hotel had to be cleansed from all the ghosts of 1994. They had to get rid of the smell of fear – from people who did not know whether they would survive to see another day. People who hoped against all hope that the international community would intervene and save their lives. Bill Clinton, back in charge after trying to cover up his liaison with Monica Lewinsky by the fateful invasion of Somalia, was the man who prevented an intervention.

The USA's stubborn refusal to declare the events in Rwanda a genocide meant that the United Nations could not intervene. This, and the fact that news teams from all over the world were concentrated in South Africa for the 1994 election meant that the 100 days it took to murder about 800 000 people in Rwanda went by almost unnoticed.

At that time the hotel was a hiding place for hundreds of refugees and was protected by a small number of UN troops stationed in the city. Some people stayed in the hotel and others slept in the garden or next to the swimming pool. But when the UN troops were withdrawn on short notice, Hutu murderers wasted no time in descending on the hotel and killing the refugees.

This was why I had such a feeling that the hotel felt clinical. They'd had to wash away and paint over the past to soften the desperate voices of the dead. At the time of our visit the hotel wasn't fully operational. Some floors still had to be repaired. The floor that I stayed on had only one side open – overlooking the swimming pool. One night I opened the door to one of the rooms that was being refurbished. I wasn't sure what I expected to see. Bullet holes in the walls? Blood on the walls? There was nothing. And when I stood in the dark room with the door closed, there was only silence. The past neatly covered with plaster so that it would not affect tourism.

Outside the hotel it was another kettle of fish. You did not have to search long and hard for stories about the genocide. It was the first item on the agenda. The Tutsis who arranged our day trips made sure of that. Have your breakfast, drink your coffee, get into the matatu and let's go look at skeletons. On the third visit to a scene related to the genocide I put my foot down. Enough was enough.

Some of the bones were still in mounds and when they removed the tarpaulins the crows flew out from underneath. Thousands of skulls made a gross exhibition on wooden shelves. Of course the impact of thousands of skulls was much bigger than the piles of bones. The rest of the bones were buried in mass graves. What happened to respect for the dead? Or was it their fate to serve as grim reminders of what happened for the rest of time?

On each tour I was given a very simplistic explanation of what happened and why. It was explained to me very slowly, as if I was a school child. The moment I started probing deeper, they explained that things aren't always what they seem. That you had to live there to understand how things worked. A little like a white South African at a dinner party in an overseas country in the 1980s.

But enough of death and philosophy. I was here to rock and roll – or at least to reggae. I was on the prowl for a party.

And prowl I did, but I sadly discovered that no amount of alcohol or disco lights could give Kigali a nightlife.

Denis, the Belgian UN representative, warned me not to expect too much. He invited me to lunch at his house in one of Kigali's best neighbourhoods, where all the diplomats lived. I hoped he would give me the names of a few interesting bars, but he wasn't of much use and on top of that the meal was a bland affair. It soon became clear that he had a hidden agenda: He wanted to meet Lucky. And after I arranged the meeting he never talked to me again.

As it became darker it also became quieter in Kigali. This was already a bad sign. Irrespective of how poor or backward any African capital city is you will always find a club that had its heyday in the late 1970s or early 1980s, but was still the life and soul of the party. It always had a pool table, a sound system that was turned up much higher than it could handle, prostitutes, and definitely Johnny Walker Black – a status drink that proved that your expensive clothes did not mean you had an empty wallet. This was the sure-fire way to distinguish the "Big Boys", as they are referred to all over the continent, from the small fry.

But in Kigali the party never started. Even the standard home shebeen kind of thing was missing here. Well, maybe not missing, but it closed very early and at first I suspected that there might be a curfew. When I saw small groups of people who hung around after sunset to enjoy a beer I soon realised that they might not be the kind of drinking companions who would do my health any good – safe pass letter or not. I don't think many of the local residents wanted to hang out with them either. The city was dead after sunset, because it was actually dangerous to be outside and people still lived in fear. Also, the police were not necessarily one's friends.

For two nights I continued my search for the nightlife with a driver who did not share my sense of adventure and excitement. The hotel itself did not offer much in the way of action and the South African musicians were, well, musos. They were travel weary and weren't interested in their surroundings. Then it hit me: in light of the lack of entertainment, I had to create my own. My grandmother always said that the devil finds work for idle hands and I'm a good example of this. Boredom always makes me get up to mischief.

One afternoon, as a result of overwhelming tedium, I took two street children to lunch at the grand Windsor Umubano Hotel. It was a most enlightening social experiment, which I undertook for purely academic reasons. The guard tried to prevent my guests from entering the hotel and the waiter refused to serve them, but I insisted, ignoring the icy atmosphere that ensued. I argued that other people were allowed to bring prostitutes to the hotel as guests and no one had a problem with that. I also demanded that we be seated at a table in the centre of the restaurant instead of one in the corner that the waiter recommended.

The restaurant wasn't full, but my fellow diners, businessmen with their expensive watches and brand new cell phones who only returned from self-imposed exile in Belgium after the genocide, were clearly not impressed with the company in which they found themselves.

The waiter addressed the two boys in Kinyarwanda and from his tone of voice I gathered that his remarks weren't complimentary. My guess was that the two boys were aged between eight and ten but they didn't take much notice of him. Suddenly they were in a position of power and no one could take it away from them. They knew I would protect them and they gave the waiter hell.

After a veritable feast of hamburgers and many Fantas some of our musicians brought their djembes and started playing their drums in the restaurant while the street children taught them Rwandese folk songs. By this time even the waiter's attitude began to change and when his manager had to leave for a few minutes he joined in the singing and showed us a few dance steps. For the first time there was a smile on his face, but it did not reach his eyes. They were still dead, hidden behind a wall around his memories.

Two hours later I accompanied the children to the hotel's exit. In the few days I'd been there I had seen how disobedient children were hit with rubber sticks. It was the norm and I wanted to prevent my new friends' day from ending badly. As we walked out the waiter breathlessly caught up with us and said something to the children in Kinyarwanda. This time there were smiles on their faces while he good-naturedly rubbed their heads.

The children walked around the block to the back of the hotel where the waiter gave each of them an enormous bag of food to take home. The image of the two boys walking down the dusty street kicking an empty sardine tin will remain with me forever, their loud and animated discussion of their afternoon adventure punctuated by carefree laughter.

It was at that point that it was decided that I was in need of a bodyguard. To this day I don't know whether it was at the insistence of the hotel or the promoter. My errant behaviour beyond the safe confines of the hotel fence, as well as inside, started to freak people out. Whether the bodyguard was appointed to protect me from other people or them from me, is open for discussion.

The important people around me did not like all my political questions and the fact that I got along with everyone made them uneasy. The last straw was when I exchanged my dollars for francs on the street and not in the hotel. I got a much better deal outside and it was much more exciting to have a forty-minute negotiation in a backstreet alley. Yes, I was busy creating my own entertainment.

I immediately christened my bodyguard "Brick". I don't know what his real name was and frankly I couldn't care. If Brick were a South African, he would have been a white rugby player who sold second-hand cars or insurance. On Saturday night after rugby games he would have hung out at escort clubs and perhaps dabbled in illegal diamonds now and then. But Brick was a much snappier dresser than his South African equivalent.

Brick always seemed to know when I'd got up in the morning and shortly after he would knock on my door. He couldn't speak English

Brick

and the only French sentence I knew wouldn't have strengthened our relationship. I forbade him to eat or drink with me. He had to get his own table, but this did not dissuade him: he even stood guard when I went to the toilet. In short, he was a first-class nuisance. He had a good laugh at all the mosquito repellents I brought along and threw them on my bed with contempt, until I told him to put them back where he got them. I soon realised that he was a feared man in the community, because people suddenly gave me a wide berth. He tried hard to act like a tourist guide rather than a policeman but his speciality was not to be too likeable.

Basically I was under hotel arrest. This dawned on me when he made himself comfortable in my hotel room under the pretext that he wanted to be my friend. Brick settled into his new role as my friend and guide by offering me his fourteen-year-old sister as a sex partner. When I strongly declined, he offered his twelve-year-old brother. This was followed by an offer of heroin, a drug that for some reason was easily available and cheap in Kigali. Heroin is a drug that magically transforms the worst situation into something good. I could understand why it was so popular, but I still found it weird.

His final offer was dagga. Now that was the best offer of the entire week.

Before I continue, I have to make a quick remark about my feelings about dagga. Dagga has caused many problems in people's lives. So have chocolate, alcohol and nicotine. Dagga is a natural plant and the only reason why it has been banned in so many places in the world is because the Americans insisted on this as part of their business agreements with several countries. Dagga is banned in America because nylon manufacturers had to get rid of the hemp plant to create a larger market for their new material.

Too much of anything is bad for you. The same applies to dagga. I look upon dagga like cognac. It's something I indulge in every now and again and really enjoy it, but I'm not interested in making it a daily habit. I like living in the real world and don't want to be removed from it constantly. One night, probably when I was stoned, I decided that because dagga comes from the soil of a country it reflects the soul of that country. I know it's a real stoner philosophy, but that's what dagga does to you.

It was time to taste the soul of Rwanda. The dagga was dark green, almost black. It left tar on your hands when you touched it. I was arrogant enough to think I was strong enough for it. Against Brick's wishes I accompanied him when he went out to buy the dagga. Only rock stars allow other people to bring them drugs and I wasn't a rock star. It also meant that I wasn't ripped off too much when it came to the price.

The seller was a guy called Richard. He wore a Hawaiian shirt, a pair of fake Ray-Bans and a gold watch that gleamed against his pitch black skin in the afternoon sun. In typical African style it was so loose around his arm that it glided up and down between his wrist and elbow. He clearly enjoyed his own stock and didn't have a problem smoking while he worked.

The fill was wrapped in a piece of newspaper. It cost 20 cents. Back in my hotel room I rolled a nice fat joint. With the first pull I already knew I was playing out of my league, but by this time I was so entrenched in my role as the arrogant white idiot who thinks Africa can't get him down, that I ignored my sixth sense. Brick's complexion also became a shade paler, but he kept his poise. When we finished the joint he left. He knew where to find me. I wasn't going anywhere.

Before he was out the door, I fell like a stone onto the bed. My body refused to obey my brain's commands. Ideas flashed through my mind at record speed, but disappeared before they could register. I was in the middle of the fastest edit I had ever seen, filled with split second images, memory flashes and visions. I saw the past, present and future all at once. As a film, it may not necessarily have received critical acclaim.

And that was the good part. Within a few minutes I was in para-noia hell. I took hold of the rest of the dagga and crawled to the bathroom to flush it down the toilet. I could already hear the police coming down the corridor. At any moment they would kick down the door and arrest me. The prospect of spending quality time in a jail cell with mass murderers awaiting trial wasn't very attractive. In Rwanda, the most macho country in Africa, inmates' uniforms are pink – probably to discourage them from escaping. No respectable man in Rwanda wants to be seen in pink in public.

I eventually succeeded in flushing the dagga. I had to keep my fist closed and hold it in the bowl while I flushed desperately to get rid of it. I could still hear the police in the corridor coming closer. The only solution was to push the bed in front of the door. In total panic I dragged the mattress from the bed, which was just a spindly frame of pressed wood, and pushed it up against the door. At last I could breathe a little easier. The enemy's first attack was averted. It was time to safeguard the perimeter further.

The window was next. On a building on the next hill, about 700 or 800 metres away, I could see a sharp-shooter who was ready to shoot me if the police couldn't break through the door. The only way to cover my view of the swimming pool was to use the mattress, which covered about two thirds of the window. I covered the rest of the window with duct tape – we all know it's bullet-proof.

Although I could still hear the voices in the corridor, I felt safer. The many voices in my head now discussed what I would do once the police burst into the room. There wasn't any dagga left and thanks to the entire can of deodorant that I sprayed into the air, I was certain they could only accuse me of spraying too much perfume in an enclosed space. Surely that would not be a crime even in such a macho country as Rwanda?

I thought about other incriminating things in my room that could lead to a stint in prison. As my brain continued to work in its uniquely disturbed way I worried that there might be very strict rules about nudity. So I tore up a photograph of my wife in her bikini and then burnt it, just in case someone tried to tape it together again.

Then, thankfully, I passed out. Twelve hours later I woke to someone hammering on my door. It was time for Lucky's show. After the concert I returned to a hotel room that was all straightened out. Nobody ever said a word.

The night before I left Kigali, Brick came to say goodbye. It wasn't a friendly farewell. He insisted on some kind of compensation for looking after me so well. It wasn't a request, it was an order. He chose my most expensive Diesel jersey. Needless to say we never became pen pals.

The sun had just set over Kigali's soccer stadium. Most of the men

in the crowd had taken off their shirts. Lucky's set went on till well after two o'clock and the audience were dripping with sweat. You could smell the crowd. In front of me 65 000 people sang: "Hey, you, Hutu man; hey, you, Tutsi man, you've got to come together as one" on the beat of Lucky's big hit "Hey, you, Rasta man; hey, you, European ..."

The concrete stadium looked like a trampoline as thousands of people jumped up and down hands in the air – one inyenzi mass that put their feelers up. People shouted exuberantly as if they needed to get rid of years of frustration. Talk about a wow moment – 65 000 people all doing primal scream therapy. The crowd got what they came for – this was one of Lucky's best concerts in years. It was impossible to hold back the tears. I looked to my left and saw all the guys from the support team quickly wiping their eyes and hoping that nobody would see them crying.

If only the preceding week had gone as smoothly. There were issues about who had to pay for meals, what sound equipment had to be used and there were problems with our transport. We had to fight for everything and nothing happened as it was supposed to. Everything was an effort. De Gaulle, the promoter, obviously felt that since Lucky and his team had arrived, it was time to begin cutting costs. But Lucky was not to be bullied.

The food and transport issues were sorted out quickly, but when De Gaulle realised that a new sound system had to be imported from Uganda because the only available sound system in Rwanda was insufficient, he became as petulant as a two-year-old child. The sound system arrived on Saturday morning, a few hours before the concert was due to start. It gave Lucky very little time for his sound check. When he arrived at the stadium about 10 000 people had already gained entry, despite clear instructions that Lucky would refuse to do a sound check if there were any people in the stadium.

They had arrived early to secure the best spots; it was not as if anybody had a job to go to.

For half an hour I tried to get the small crowd out of the stadium. From the middle of an empty stage I shouted instructions over the microphone, but I was greeted by silence. There was no way they were going to take me seriously. Nobody moved an inch. I'd like to think that the fact that they were French speaking and that I addressed them in English explains why they ignored me. I didn't even get the sarcastic applause that you'd expect to get in South Africa if you tried the same trick.

After years of managing concerts I knew I was fighting a losing battle. So I discussed our dilemma with the promoter, but in a matter of milliseconds he lost his ability to understand English. I then went to the head of security who merely shrugged in a very French way, rolled his eyes skywards and continued the conversation he was having with someone else. I felt completely helpless. Was there no respect for white people in Africa anymore?

There are two kinds of policemen in Rwanda. One group looked like refugees in their badly fitted green uniforms and no one took them seriously – or at least not until they whacked you over the head for no apparent reason. The other group wore black uniforms, never took off their sunglasses and carried automatic weapons. People avoided them like the plague, nobody even looked at them. They were almost like the Johannesburg Metro Police, only worse. They even smelled like evil.

At first I did not consider approaching them even though they were responsible for security in the back stage area. But finally, at my wits end, I explained the situation to their commander.

He got onto the stage and spoke just two sentences. Within seconds there was a stampede to get out of the stadium. Problem solved. The concert could go ahead.

After less than a week in Rwanda I started to understand how things worked.

In fact, after surviving Rwandese dagga, Brick the Bodyguard and possible death by boredom, I could begin to imagine a future as a modern day Livingstone. I decided that it was not time to go home yet and that I should stay a while longer. I wanted to explore Africa's most densely populated country. After all my hard work it was time for a holiday.

Upon my arrival in Rwanda I received a letter from the man who was appointed "security chief" for Lucky's tour. The letter was a safe pass and clearly stated that anyone who even thought of messing with me would be held accountable by the forceful, albeit slightly overworked, Rwandese legal system. I had my own "get out of jail free" card and for once, I felt like a very powerful man.

When the security chief wanted it back a week or two later, I knew it was time to leave. With his dead eyes and face pockmarked by hand granade shrapnel he was no oil painting. He was a secretive ex-secret policeman who didn't reveal much about his background. A few days later our once jovial relationship took a drastic turn for the worse when in a drunken stupor he almost sent me home in a wooden box...

Back in the good old days Gisenyi's weather and its lake was a big draw card for rich colonialists and local businessmen who wanted to let off a little steam. Actually, if you were one of the chosen few, things have always been great in Rwanda. This small town in the northwestern part of Rwanda was also the entry point for missionaries, ransackers and other adventurers into the war-torn, anarchistic eastern part of the Democratic Republic of the Congo (DRC). To Livingstone Maas it sounded like the ideal holiday spot.

Tourist brochures describe Rwanda as the land of a thousand hills. I wouldn't know if there are exactly a thousand, but there were enough. Kigali itself is situated on a central highland. Any travelling inevitably entails incessant ups and downs and because there are no railway lines, *all* transport is by road. On top of that, only 9% of the 13 500 kilometres of road in Rwanda is tarred. Mercifully the road I was on was part of the 9%.

Bicycles and heavily laden trucks, unroadworthy buses and pedestrians all competed for a spot on the narrow road that wound its way through the jungle to Gisenyi. And the jungle was fighting a determined battle to take over the road. Most of the time two vehicles could scarcely pass each other. In a situation like this, most reasonable people would slow down to avoid metal scratching against metal, but Rwandese drivers didn't get that. They drove as fast as possible, hooting at anything smaller than them, and making it the other driver's problem to avoid carnage.

The range of interesting scratches along the side of the bus attested to the fact that our driver's life's mission was to knock down as many cyclists as he could. As the bus did not have a television set, he took it as his personal responsibility to entertain his passengers. He was supposed to, but never hooted when he was about to pass someone on a bicycle. Each time he scraped someone, a few ringleaders in the bus jeered excitedly. I could understand why life expectancy in Rwanda is only 48.

Would I shut my eyes to this irresponsible game or be the outsider who interferes? It didn't take me long to take out my safe pass and shove it under the driver's nose. I told him to stop his games. He was surprised, but decided to listen to me. The rest of the passengers didn't speak to me again. Were they angry with me or afraid of me?

I knew there was only one real city in Rwanda, so I didn't expect much from Gisenyi. What I found was a shanty town. Some of the streets were tarred and the few shops were all built in the Belgian colonial style of architecture with lean-tos and columns. Some were painted and it was clear that blue was the overwhelmingly favourite colour. Advertisements for Primus beer brightened the otherwise drab buildings. Hundreds of people braved the roads on Chinese motorcycles that swarmed through the streets like demented killer bees.

It was possible to hire someone with an umbrella who would walk with you, providing shade against the harsh sun. You could also rent bicycles with wooden wheels to carry your shopping home. It might

have been illegal to exchange money on the streets in Kigali, but here it was done openly through wooden shutters. Tailors advertised their wares next to the road in true African style and colourful French adverts tried to entice would-be shoppers. Children had their fun by mixing up Muslims' shoes outside the mosque.

Gisenyi was a thoroughfare into the Congo. My first feeling was one of a frontier town in the Wild West. I waited with bated breath for the sheriff to throw a troublemaker out of the bar. As we drove into the town, I involuntary started whistling the theme song of *The Good, The Bad and The Ugly*. For the first time in hours my fellow passengers took notice of me again.

The Izuba Hotel was a big surprise. The lawn, which always looks greener and lusher in the tropics than anywhere else was neatly cut. The garden consisted of a variety of interesting plants, trees and flowers I had never seen before. The swimming pool was big and perfectly blue. From the swimming pool the lake shimmered in the distance like a gem. A layer of mist over the lake made the mountains, a good 100 kilometres away, look like a water-colour painting from a master's hand.

The hotel, which was in good order, had to have another use than only housing holidaymakers. I discovered my fellow guests were indeed mercenaries, prostitutes and blood diamond traders. There were anti-aircraft guns on the roof, sandbags at the entrance and armed soldiers in all the public spaces of the hotel. They weren't there for a rowdy party. The Wild West was closer than I thought.

I soon found out how explosive Gisenyi really was when I started a riot on my first visit to the local market. Before I set out on my journey I decided to take a series of photographs of children. I was spellbound by the eyes of the Rwandan children whose gaze was much older than befitted their young faces and bodies. Many of them had marks on their necks caused by blunt hacking-knives. As medical assistance was out of the question during the genocide, the skin grew over the open wound, taking on the appearance of a gutted prawn.

Everywhere I went in Rwanda I asked children whether I could take photographs of them. Now and then a child said no, but in general they granted my request. In Gisenyi it was another story; no one wanted their photo taken. A possible explanation could have been the fact that thousands of Hutus were housed in refugee camps just across the border.[1] Among the refugees were members of the Interahamwe, the Hutu militia who led the genocide. They weren't refugees in the true sense of the word and were busy regrouping. People feared what might still happen in the near future – and a photograph could be used to identify you.

The rubbish-littered market reflected the town's economic status. The products were aimed at the impoverished masses and the stalls specialised in cheap Chinese flip-flops and second-hand clothes from Europe. The market was held on a large open piece of ground without any protection against the sun. Pieces of raw meat were covered by a thick crust of flies. It was only after a day or so that someone took me to a storage place where thousands of local art works, carved bone, fetish dolls, witch-doctor goodies, elephant tusks, hippopotamus teeth, leopard skins and gorilla hands were on sale.

At the market I asked a few children whether I could take their photograph, but without success. Then a bashful teenage boy with a wooden bicycle approached me and asked whether I wanted to take his photograph. He was older than the other children I had photographed so far, but it would have been rude to say no. After I took the photo I gave him the equivalent of R2. Within moments

---

1 The 1994 genocide was instigated by the Hutus and lasted about four months. It was brought to an end when a Tutsi rebel group, the Rwandan Patriotic Front, defeated the Hutu-controlled army. Because they feared the Tutsis' revenge thousands of Hutus fled to the Congo. They were interned in refugee camps, which caused another humanitarian crisis.

another boy was next to him, trying to grab his R2. I was dumb-founded. All of a sudden I was a spectator at a fist fight that quickly escalated into a full-blown wrestling match. Everyone around me began shouting hysterically.

The market, which had been quiet and fairly empty up until then, suddenly swarmed with people. It was as if some animal instinct took over. Nobody knew what the fighting was about, but every-one wanted to be part of it. And I'm not talking about four or five people – from nowhere a group of about 60 people appeared and gathered around us.

The fighting was relentless and as the accidental instigator I felt I had to do something about it, but there was no way that I could try to break up the fight. Then I saw a knife glistening in the sunlight. The situation had become too hardcore for me. Seconds later I heard automatic gunfire as a lorry with soldiers rounded the corner at breakneck speed.

I noticed a movement to my left. A taxi driver opened his door: "Time for you to go," he said. I did not argue and never returned to the market. The trip to the hotel, which was shorter than a kilometre, cost me 50 dollars.

The hotel was a nice enough place, but as in Kigali there was not much to do there. After the first day the prostitutes realised that I wasn't a potential client and left me alone. I relaxed next to the swimming pool and paddled about in the glistening lake, accompa-nied by an armed guard. I initiated conversations with mercenaries and diamond smugglers in the bar.

One night, after a few stiff drinks, one of the diamond dealers showed me the contents of his reinforced Adidas sports bag. It was half-filled with diamonds. The next day I saw him boarding a smoking aircraft in dire need of a service on an untarred runway just outside town. The same night he returned with more diamonds. Several days later I recognised him when he walked through customs and

immigration at OR Tambo with the same bag. No one investigated
its contents.

For some reason the security chief who issued me the safe pass took
a liking to me. Out of the blue he arrived in Gisenyi to see what I
was up to. He had an interesting proposal: Would I like to see what
the DRC looked like?

Gisenyi's neighbouring town is Goma. In actual fact, it's more or
less the same town with a passport control point in the centre. At
that time, as today, the eastern part of the Congo was a mess. There
were so many rebel factions that nobody knew who was on whose
side. Sometimes they didn't even know themselves.

Gisenyi didn't have any nightlife. Every night I could hear the
parties in Goma while I searched for an English channel on television. I was a frustrated party animal. The security chief's offer was
tempting, but I told him that I did not have a visa for the DRC. He
said it was not a problem, since Rwanda controlled much of that
region, and that he could organise that I go through without one.
He wanted to show me exactly how powerful he was.

To spend a day with the gorillas in the mountains would have
cost $500, but I couldn't afford that. What it would cost to see the
guerrillas wasn't clear yet, but at least I was about to find out.

The road that linked Gisenyi and Goma was obstructed by a single
cross-bar. The soldiers who manned the control point took a great
deal of pleasure in taunting everyone who wanted to go through.
Here they played God as they decided who could go through and who
could not. Women were pawed and men humiliated to make sure
everyone knew who was boss. Strangely enough, it did not seem to
bother most people – they accepted that this was how things worked.

The soldiers didn't exactly look fighting fit, but they were certainly well armed. Each of them carried that all too popular symbol
of power in Africa: the AK47. They prodded people into rows with

the barrels. Some were called out of the line and taken around the corner for interrogation. The people who stood in the rows did not make eye contact and looked steadfastly at the ground. Even if the person in front or behind them was pushed around, they did not show any reaction.

When I got to the front, the security chief ordered me to leave my passport at the control point. My courage failed me. This was flagrantly disregarding the number one rule of international travel – you should always have your passport on you. "I'm the boss here. You leave passport. We pick up when we come back," he barked at me. I doubted the wisdom of my decision, but I had to concede even if it was unwillingly.

Goma and Gisenyi may be sister towns, but they certainly had different fathers. A different set of rules applied in each of the two towns. Although no road or river linked Kinshasa and Goma, it was still more Congolese than Rwandese. Goma was a bustling little town. There were cars and taxis and street café's and pool tables where people drank beer. The roads were in an even worst condition than those in Gisenyi.

The town smelled strange and "dark" in a way, something I attributed to a flight of fancy before I realised there were active volcanoes close by. This also explained the dirty, black layer of silt that covered everything.

Our first stop was a local bar where the security chief shooed people away from a table so that we could sit down. It was ten o'clock in the morning. The table was vintage plastic garden furniture; the walls were unpainted and for drinks you could choose between whisky, gin or cognac. South Africa was represented by Amarula and Castle. The security chief explained loudly and with large gestures how Goma and the countryside surrounding it also belonged to Rwanda. The locals looked at him with disdain, but he didn't give a damn. He was Mr Big Shot and no one would be able to burst his bubble.

There were huge petrol depots for vehicle and aircraft fuel. The explosion I'd heard a few nights previously at the Izuba Hotel happened at one of the depots. Apparently someone tried to steal fuel and the soldiers shot at him. The thief and the soldiers all died in the explosion. The thief's burnt body was still lying there, his arms outstretched as if in a final plea to God. Nobody seemed terribly bothered by the corpse and the security chief regarded its presence as a very public warning to others not to steal. "These people …" he said, while he waved his arm with loathing over the town. He definitely wasn't there to win friends and influence people.

The official reason for the presence of Rwandan troops in the eastern part of the Congo was to prevent another attack by the Interahamwe, whose members had fled to those parts. In theory they were safeguarding the entire area against them. In reality Rwanda was a poor country and the eastern part of the Congo was every capitalist's dream. Its natural resources were a big draw card for all kinds of entrepreneurs. There were diamonds in abundance and their most important mineral was used to manufacture tin. While the Rwandan troops were busy "safeguarding" that area, they were also busy with large-scale theft to fill their own and their government's coffers. You could see the signs of prosperity everywhere: gold watches, new cars and shiny shoes that were wiped clean every so often.

A few beers later the security chief decided it was time to move on for lunch. He did his fellow boozers proud – by this time he'd already had half a bottle of whisky. I seriously doubted that we would get a decent meal in this war-torn town. He pushed the nose of his Toyota 4x4 (another standard issue in many parts of Africa) in a westerly direction. The town became a jungle for a few kilometres until high walls unexpectedly rose up next to us. The entrance to the premises was packed with sandbags and there were soldiers carrying Brownings.

We entered a magical world. A beautiful, snow-white colonial house commanded our attention. Kilometres of lawn were neatly mowed and the garden was manicured up to the edge of the lake where luxurious yachts and speedboats worth hundreds of thousands of rand bobbed in the water. The waiters wore waistcoats and their bowties and starched cloths worn across their arms were brand-new. Here you would not see any signs of war, only the people who benefited from it in a big way. I even spotted a Hummer in the parking area.

The lunch menu wasn't complicated. You could choose between pizza, pizza and pizza at 40 American dollars a piece. The cheapest whisky was Johnny Walker Blue. The pizza crust tasted like bread and the cheese was hardly visible over the half-baked effort. Around me everyone feasted. How else did one spend the spoils of war?

Everyone always tells you that "there is no such a thing as a free lunch" and this valuable lesson I learnt in Goma's country club. The security chief got drunker and drunker and more people joined us at our table to be introduced to the brave mzungu. The next moment someone got out a television camera. The same television team who had waited for us at the Kigali airport, reappeared in Goma and suddenly wanted to interview me.

Then it struck me what the invitation was really about. The plan was to show that Rwanda had had such success in cleaning up those parts of the Congo that it was safe enough for a white tourist to lunch there. I agreed to the interview, but I talked so much politics and went into such detail about how Rwanda was stealing the Congo's resources that I doubt it was ever used.

I was ready to go home, or at least back to Gisenyi. I had had enough exposure to Big Boy's arrogance and people who benefited from other's misery. The pizza didn't do much to lift my spirits either and the beers began to affect my better judgement.

But Mr Security Chief, quite peeved that his PR stunt had not gone according to plan, had more up his sleeve. He was intent on showing me exactly how far his influence extended into the Congo and rejected any resistance on my part. He had the keys and I was at his mercy. Armed with another bottle of whisky for the road he drove in a westerly direction and we went deeper into the war zone.

We got through the first roadblock without any trouble. The second one was bad enough to make my urgent need to pee disappear and the third one was the cherry on top. At the third roadblock Mr Security Chief, in his drunken arrogance, got involved in a brawl with a soldier who was even drunker than he was. He insisted on being let through, but the soldier was set on stopping him.

The soldier's uniform was decorated with freaky fetish symbols that would make any sane person tremble. A split second after he put his AK47 rifle through the open window at the security chief's side, I was already standing next to the vehicle. My beer pee was back and more pressing than ever. I could not wait for the outcome of their fight; I *had* to go and walked into the bushes. I had just opened my fly, when I saw a man sleeping in the grass. That was very strange, especially given everything that was going on only a few metres away. I stepped closer to inspect him and then I saw the small, round hole in the centre of his forehead. I nearly wet myself. He would never wake up again.

When I looked around I realised there were seven or eight more bodies. I didn't hang around for an exact body count or to find out if they were all indeed dead. But I did grasp immediately where the fighting at the roadblock was leading. I ran back to the bakkie to find the security chief standing next to the vehicle with his pistol against the soldier's head and the soldier's AK47 against his. I began to plead with them and took the bottle of whisky from the bakkie as a peace offering for the soldier. I had some success in calming everyone down and at last I got the security chief back into the bakkie. At that point I demanded to GO BACK IMMEDIATELY. The details of that particular conversation were lost in the adrenaline of the moment.

I regained consciousness when we entered Goma just after sunset, where the security chief demanded another beer. I could see the lights of my hotel beyond the security post. I left him there and had a huge fight at the control point until my passport was back in my hands. The next morning the security chief – who clearly didn't sleep a wink – woke me with an incessant knocking on my door. By then the whisky bottle looked like a natural extension of his hand. He wanted his safe pass letter.

A few hours later I was on an aircraft back to South Africa. Nyiragongo, the volcano near Goma erupted some years later. For some reason the lava missed Gisenyi, but flattened Goma. I secretly hoped that a certain security chief was busy drinking there when it happened.

The Rwandan anthem is entitled *Rwanda Nziza,* which means "Rwanda the beautiful". In Zulu *siza* means to help or aid someone. I have always found the similarity between these two words very ironic.

# HONEYMOONING IN AFRICA
## Madagascar, 1999

**F**IFTEEN MINUTES BEFORE our Air Madagascar flight was due to land in Antananarivo, the pilot cleared this throat for an announcement. My first thought was that they had discovered another box of French champagne, since we had already finished off the allocation that came with breakfast.

Air Madagascar had clearly underestimated the unquenchable thirst of the group of South African tourists and musicians it had on board that morning. The breakfast bubbly put everyone in a jovial mood and some of the passengers walked around in the half empty economy class section striking up conversations with strangers. In the back of the aeroplane Johnny Clegg's band puffed away at their smokes while their lead singer, like a true rock star, travelled first class.

One of the quirks of my job as a record company executive was the daily intrusion of musicians. When my wife Pauli and I realised at the airport that the band was also on our flight, Pauli's body language was easy to read. She just shook her head as if to say, "will-I-ever-get-rid-of-these-people?" But this time, for a change, we wouldn't be bothered by the musicians.

Somehow Johnny's bass guitar player found out that we were on honeymoon and asked the air hostesses to make it public knowledge.

After the announcement everybody sang raucously, including Johnny's background singers who lent some degree of musicality to the song. The rest of the well-wishers sang with wild abandon. It wasn't even twelve o'clock yet.

Madagascar here we come.

Pauli and I weren't exactly traditional honeymooners. Both of us had been married before and had made up our minds never to do it again. We lived in sin for many happy years. Our three children from our previous marriages viewed the matter a little differently. They were embarrassed because they did not know how to introduce us to their friends (the friends who were allowed to visit them – some parents forbade their children to hang out at the House of Sin).

When we eventually did decide to get married, a few storms threatened to disrupt our beach wedding at Hermanus. The timing couldn't have been worse. The death of Pauli's parents in a car crash two months before the wedding didn't exactly put us in a festive mood. Her eldest brother, a fully-fledged recluse, had to be dragged to Hermanus kicking and screaming. On the day, my grandmother refused to brave the windy conditions on the beach and my mother was upset that a minister did not perform the ceremony.[2] Sibling rivalry also reached an all time high. When asked to say something, my youngest son blessed us by saying: "I wish you were still married to my mother."

The final straw was arriving at the hotel we'd chosen for our wedding night and finding it still under construction. The only highlight was my father's wedding gift – a vacation to Madagascar, which we would only get around to taking a year later.

There is one benefit to being divorced and that is that you can

---

2  We asked a guy with a long beard in a caftan who lived in India for years, but refused to belong to any faith, doctrine or specific philosophy to marry us.

send the children to your ex every second Christmas and rekindle the romance in your current marriage. In December 1999 we all thought the world would come to a grinding halt when the next century dawned. The tickets were cheap and the children were at the exes – it was time for a romantic tropical getaway.

The only thing was that I'm not that into traditional holidays. I hate being a typical tourist and I have a particular problem with group holidays and package tours. I'd rather stay on a few days after a business visit and use my local contacts to have a more personalised experience. I also detest hanging out with other tourists, especially other South Africans. At home I scarcely get along with most of them. Why would I spend time with them in foreign parts? Also, how often does a man get the chance to sit down in a bar and talk to his wife about their sex life without anyone understanding what you are saying?

Pauli's dream vacation destination was unspoilt, preferably with long, white beaches and a warm ocean, good food and as few people as possible. My ideal holiday was to visit a foreign city, try out their local beer and party until the small hours of the night to the sound of local music. Our "honeymoon" (five years after we moved in together and a year after we got married) therefore had to meet specific requirements. We eventually found a happy medium. The first part of the holiday was booked at Île Sainte-Marie, also known as Nosy Boraha, an island about an hour's flight east of Madagascar. This was Pauli's part of the holiday.

Then we would spend a week exploring the nightlife of Antananarivo (Tana for short) as my part of the holiday. Those in the know say that a successful marriage means that you should leave your ego at the front door without giving up your personality. They also say that a good marriage requires compromise. If that was true, we had an extremely successful marriage.

For some reason Madagascar does not really feature on South

Africans' list of vacation destinations. Not sure why. It's cheaper than Cape Town and their food ranks among the best in Africa. Maybe South Africans are afraid to make spelling mistakes, because your spelling capabilities will certainly be tested in Madagascar. The word for impressed, a formidable word in Afrikaans too, is the awe-inspiring "mampipendrampendrana". The name of the Madagascan king who ruled between 1787 and 1810 was Anrianampoinimeri-nandriantsimitovianminandriampanjaka. If you were a close friend, you were allowed to call him Andrianampoinimerina.

The Malagasy grammatical rules were compiled by a language group just as infamous for their spelling rules: the Welsh. When Welsh missionaries tried to recreate the spoken language into a written language, they had to contort the alphabet around a language that was a concoction of Malagasy, English and French. The letters c, q, u, w and x didn't even exist in the Malagasy alphabet. Don't think you'll be able to pick up the language in a week and pass yourself off as a local.

Something else that makes Madagascar so special is the fact that it has been floating around in the ocean by its lonesome self for such a long time. Of the 200 000 endemic fauna and flora, 150 000 are peculiar to the island. I'm not much of a nature lover, but some things were so weird that even I was fascinated – flying apes, frogs the size of your thumb that jump up and down in perfect sync in troops of 10 000, and of course the bats. I have always thought bats are proof that God likes horror movies, because I can't think of another reason why He would have made them.

If you hire a guide to search for flying lemurs in one of the national parks, you'll be sure to find an important item in his backpack. And if you expected it to be a first-aid kit with all the right muti for poisonous snakes bites and the like, you would be dead wrong.

Lemurs are nocturnal and extremely territorial. So in your guide's backpack you'll find a small cassette recorder and a tape with sounds of another group of lemurs. When he plays this among a group of sleeping lemurs, they immediately wake up, ready to protect their area. A group of rudely awakened lemurs make a cacophony of sound. It is beyond scary and of course highly illegal, but I promised our guide that my lips were sealed.

The Madagascan population is almost as diverse and unique as its fauna and flora. About 165 million years ago the island splintered off from Africa and it took a leisurely 45 million years to travel the 500 kilometres to its existing coordinates in the Indian Ocean. The first inhabitants were Indonesian or Malay. Black Africans arrived later and even later the Arabs, Chinese and Indians joined the party. The last arrivals were the French who colonised the entire lot. Their language is the only uniting factor.

Tana's airport design is pure genius. The terminal doors open onto the runway. When an aeroplane takes off, they first have to close the doors to prevent the heat from the plane's turbine from incinerating the people inside the airport building. Our tour guide, Kenny, who earns a meagre R150 a month, advised that we exchange enough money before we set off for Île Sainte-Marie. At that time there were only a few places on the small island where one could exchange money and nobody accepted travellers' cheques. Our R4 000 bought us so many Madagascan francs that I had to stuff them into different bags.

As there weren't any reserved seats on the flight to Île Sainte-Marie, everyone descended on the small prop-jet plane like a swarm of locusts. As we stepped into the plane we had to hand in our boarding passes because the airline wanted to use them for the next flight. There was a stack of newspapers in the aircraft – all of them in Malagasy or French. I studied the photographs intently without realising that this would be the start of a vacation-long search for English reading matter. Later I had the good fortune to buy five-day-old English newspapers on the street. Entrepreneurs recycled the newspapers they found in hotel rooms or aeroplanes by neatly pressing them before they sold them at exorbitant prices to news hungry visitors such as moi.

With nothing to read I lost myself in the indigo Indian Ocean far below. Maybe the distinctly French flavour of the country was rubbing off on me, but I started getting visions of a nude romp with my wife on a remote beach. Suddenly the idea of a week in the middle of nowhere was more appealing. After years together this was our first real holiday. My initial irritation that my cell phone didn't work was long forgotten. I fell asleep dreaming of the two of us frolicking in the shallow waves like Burt Lancaster and Deborah Kerr in *From Here to Eternity*.

I awoke during the rocky landing on the short runway of Île Sainte-Marie's airport. The arrivals hall was a small wooden building and the airport personnel were dressed in shorts and sandals. A large group of children dressed in tatters crowded around us asking for *stilos* and *bon-bons*[3].

The air smelled fresh. It was the scent of coconuts … the fragrance of the tropics. I stretched, looked up and saw a cloudless sky framed by palm branches. The other South African tourists were no longer with us — they fell for the shiny brochures and package options of the resorts on Madagascar's main island. At last I would be able to speak Afrikaans without anyone understanding me.

My mouth was dry. It was time for a beer.

---

3  At first I thought they were trying to sell me some dagga, but I found out later that "stilo" is the French word for pen and "bon-bon" is a sweet.

We were picked up in a 4x4, while the other tourists were collected by a minibus. We would shortly find out why. Our first stop was Ambodifotatra, the main town on Île Sainte-Marie. Wooden huts on poles lined the dirt road. Most houses didn't have doors, just brightly printed material in front of the opening, which let in a light breeze. There were no glass windows, only wooden shutters to keep out the rain.

The shebeen-like bars don't have tables and no one sits inside. You get a small chair, put your beer bottle on the ground and watch the cars cruise by in slow motion to avoid the potholes.

Three Horses beer has been a Madagascan institution since the fifties. The origin of the name remains a mystery, because there aren't any horses on the island. But then again, you need not live in a mansion to enjoy a Castle. In Madagascar, as on the rest of the continent, beer is sold in 750ml bottles. So while your friends are trying to keep you on your feet and you're trying your utmost to focus, you can tell your wife in all honesty that you've only had four beers. Remember not to get mixed up and order a White Horses, unless you want to get the "has-this-guy-gone-bonkers?" look from the barman.

After a couple of beers the hotel's 4x4, loaded with gallon drums of diesel and other provisions, stopped in front of the bar. The 30 kilometres to the hotel would take us longer than two hours, but until then we were still blissfully unaware of this fact. The map indicated a road to the hotel, but in reality it was hardly more than a dry ditch.

Pauli was so excited about her tropical vacation that she decided to leave all her bras at home. We were in for a bumpy ride, and an exasperated Pauli had to use one hand to press against the roof of the vehicle and the other to try and contain her boobs. After the Three Horses I found it hilarious and could not wait for the next donga, but all credit to the driver and his passenger who kept poker faces during the entire trip.

It seemed that the road would be reclaimed by the lush tropical vegetation if given half a chance. A few wooden houses next to the road anxiously stood their ground, but the jungle was waiting for someone to go away for the weekend to retrieve what was rightfully his. But in Madagascar, where the average annual income is less than the cost of a meal in a local hotel, nobody goes away for the weekend.

We reached paradise just after a spectacular sunset. Our travelling time of more than twelve hours was starting to take its toll and I could feel a headache coming on from all the drinking during the day. It was stifling hot with little variation in the day and night temperature. I gulped down the complimentary welcome drink, ran to the beach while tearing off my clothes and dashed into the moonlit sea. The water was tepid, but I was already experiencing something new. Then I stepped onto something that almost went right through my foot. What can I say? Fools rush in where angels fear to tread.

I woke up with a swollen foot and a thudding headache. It could have been my hangover. I still had no idea what I stepped on, but I decided that I would wear my sandals for all future swims.

People say that the tropics smell stuffy, but it's a pleasant smell and not the same as city stuffiness. It smells of rotten leaves and although it doesn't have the same effect as air freshener, at least it's natural. It's heavy, but charming. It's not a fragrance that could be bottled easily. Pauli always says that you'll be attracted to something or someone if you like their smell. I understood that now. I liked the smell of Île Sainte-Marie.

In the early morning we realised we were truly in Eden. One step took us from our porch to the beach. The beautiful sandy coastline shaded by coconut palms stretched for kilometres in both directions like a silky white ribbon and the only signs of life were ducks paddling in the shallow water. The placid azure water seemed to go on forever.

Our wooden hut was on poles to direct the storm water of regular cyclones underneath the hut. The roof was made of banana leaves.

The hotel consisted of rustic wooden huts serving as the office and a kitchen, and a slightly larger hut with a broad veranda around it was the bar and restaurant. During breakfast you had to order your lunch so that the staff could catch or slaughter what you'd chosen. Crayfish, fresh fish, shrimps and duck were all prepared by a French trained chef. One day I walked into the kitchen and caused the untimely death of a chicken by asking whether I could have some chicken. The chef looked out of the window before he replied: "Yes!"

But I can honestly not recommend the chicken, as they are super free range and consequently way too muscular. I was told that Madagascar has a strong Indonesian influence and that the absence of cats should serve as a warning to anyone who would like to order meat in a restaurant – unless it's clearly indicated as "zebu", Malagasy for beef. Oh, and brace yourself for lots of vanilla.

We spent our days lazing around on the beach, eating, swimming with the locals and drinking punch coco. Punch coco is a combination of home-brewed rum and coconut milk. It's a perfect drink with lunch since it gets you in the siesta mood in no time.

While it only took us a few hours to get used to the local drinks, certain Madagascan customs will always seem somewhat bizarre … like the way they bury their dead. The rule is that children may not inherit anything when their father dies. Everything he owns is sold after his death and a huge party is held. When the party is over, the deceased is laid to rest in a wooden corral. The body is not buried, but lies beneath a pile of soil. Everything that was consumed at the burial party, from cattle heads to empty liquor bottles are then displayed on top of the heap. If you were really well off, an artist carves statues from wood that depict your life story. These are then displayed around your grave.

In other instances the head of the family is buried in something resembling a small cave and it is closed off with a round stone that can be rolled away. If someone in town dreams of that person, which happens every five years or so, they collect the dead man's bones, dress him in new clothes and carry the whole lot around in a piece of cloth. After a few outings the bones are returned to the cave. The family has to pay for everything and the idea is that it will keep the ancestors happy.

There were a few of these cave-like graves in Île Sainte-Marie, but it was the pirates' graves that really fired my imagination. The island's biggest claim to fame is that it was once a centre for pirates. You can only reach the pirate cemetery during low tide and only at certain times of the year. The pirates' gravestones are easily recognisable thanks to the skull and crossed bones carved into them.

I have had an affinity for pirates since I was a child and long before Johnny Depp immortalised Captain Jack Sparrow. This was the playground of big names like William Kidd and Thomas Tew who contributed to the island's gene pool. Standing at the graves, you can't help but admire these guys who explored the new world while plundering ships laden with riches. When local guides take tourists to the cemetery, they always leave *bon-bons* on their gravestones. They think it's necessary to appease the pirates' spirits because they're disturbing them for financial gain but somehow I don't think the pirates would have a problem with it.

Reliving the island's pirate history occupied me for a day, but the idleness soon got to me. I started feeling like a typical tourist and that's never a good thing for me. When I'm bored and restless, I tend to create situations that will lead to entertainment and action. It was time to release my Don King persona.

But then we succeeded in doing the most touristy thing possible – we rented bicycles to explore the island. Before I continue, I have to mention that apart from wild animals, I have a complete aversion to exercise. Only major boredom would drive me to this point, but if the island was good enough for the pirates before me, there had to be something in it for me too. We packed our food supplies: Tasty sweet bread sandwiches, water, a bottle of Three Horses and punch coco. By this time Pauli, who tans easily, had red bikini tan lines over her body. As usual I was dressed in SPF 750.

Also, my vision of a nude romp with my wife on a tropical beach still hadn't come true. The Madagascans are very conservative and we were warned early on that the locals frown upon improper behaviour on the beach. However, I wasn't willing to give up on my dream just yet.

The previous evening Pauli and I played poker in the bar and made up our own rules where we could win favours from each other. Pauli is usually rather stingy with her favours. If you're married to someone who gets bored easily, it's a good way to ensure the future of the relationship. The balmy weather, the fact that we could bet in Afrikaans and the effect of the punch coco made her more adventurous than usual.

A quick rewind: When I got 80% in Sub A, my dad bought me a camera. And I have been taking photographs ever since. I would have become a photographer if my parents hadn't insisted that I get a degree to have "something to fall back on". Many people of my generation will have a similar tale to tell.

When you combine a love for photography with a companion who hates being photographed, it leads to unnecessary frustration and confrontation. I fell in love with the only woman on the planet who doesn't like being photographed. Fortunately, I had a strong poker hand and won a huge favour. Pauli – *sans* clothes – had to pose on the beach while I photographed her.

So, the idea was that we should take a leisurely ride, see how far we got and what we could experience along the way. The next day we had an early start and soon the punch coco was in much higher demand than the sandwiches. But then crisis struck.

My bicycle chain broke at exactly the farthest turning point from the hotel and I could not even phone the AA to tow me. I have a long-standing hate of bicycles. You always have to push them up a hill, your coccyx becomes quite numb and then the chain breaks or you get a flat tyre at the least opportune moment.

The only reason why we decided on the bicycles was because our transport options on the island were limited. You could get along either by foot, bicycle or motorbike. Carried away by idyllic island living, I naively thought that a bicycle would be a more romantic option than a motorbike. It is a mistake that I'm not likely to repeat soon. There I was, stranded in the bundu with a sensitive backside, empty stomach and a useless bicycle that I had to push back all the way to the hotel. I feverishly prayed that *Star Trek*'s teleporter would magically appear to dematerialise us and rematerialise us back in our room.

But then I got what I asked for and the shot of excitement that followed was nearly enough to last me for the remainder of our island holiday. On our way back we met a man who wore a black suit, complete with a white shirt, tie and back hat. He looked like a church elder and also pushed his bicycle. I was dressed in shorts and sandals and sweated profusely. It seemed that the man in the suit was moving around in an air-conditioned bubble. He was unmistakably a long-time acclimatised local. He was dignified and exuded a presence that elevated him above the other inhabitants with their bare feet and torn T-shirts left behind by tourists.

The Elder was the local history teacher and his knowledge of South African history astounded us. Although he was interested in the history of the freedom struggle, his field of speciality was the history of the National Party. He believed Frederik Willem de Klerk – he never just used his initials – was the greatest statesman who has ever lived.

As he lived on a remote island, Pauli and I decided that it would only be right to inform him what had transpired in South Africa during the past five years (keep in mind this was 1999). In simple English we told him about the changes, that the Nats handed power to the ANC and that everyone could vote. Very chuffed with myself I told him about Mandela, the rainbow nation and the Rugby World Cup in 1995.

The Elder tilted his head while he listened. At the end of my story a frown crinkled his face.

"Whyyoutellingmethis?" he fired at me, no pauses between his words.

"Well, we now have a new president and a free country."

"Iamnotchild," he chided. "Iknowallthesethings. IknowMandelaandtheANCandFrederikWillemdeKlerkisstillthegreateststatesmanofalltimes."

I realised The Elder had already decided that no tourist with bad dress sense would convince him otherwise. After politely lifting his hat to Pauli he got on his bicycle. He was probably on his way to do more research about Frederik Willem de Klerk.

Pauli and I were dumbstruck and doubted the surreal appearance. Was he a hallucination? Even the president of Madagascar was hardly seen in a suit. Our experience was like something out of a David Lynch production, possibly *Twin Peaks*. How did The Elder gain all this knowledge about FW? And why? The answers to all my questions disappeared down the road with the lone black figure.

Slowly making our way back, we went in search of the waterfall on the island. And if we had known that "cascade" was the French word for waterfall we would have found it much sooner. Afterwards it was patently obvious, but the crude signs with the word "cascade" decorated with blood and chicken feathers did not give us the sense that we were on the right track. When we eventually found it, we first drank warm Fanta and ate Tiko soup with the inhabitants of Tanambao. Then the whole town joined us for a swim. All five of them. The waterfall's water provided the only cold swim of the holiday.

On the way back from the waterfall I decided to collect my poker debt. I'm a firm believer that all bets should be honoured, irrespective how small or obscure they may be. We walked down to a small bay close to the waterfall; it was a picture perfect spot. Here I clicked away to my heart's content while Pauli played in the shallow water without a stitch of clothing. My photographs might not have made the cut for Sports Illustrated's swimsuit edition, but I was very pleased. My dreams for an island holiday came true, even though my suggestion for an imitation in the nude of the scene in *From Here to Eternity* was rejected.

Afterwards we sat on a dune and enjoyed the view of the bay. There was no one in sight and there was an almost tangible silence – even the ocean was quiet. For the first time I understood what Pauli meant when she said that nothing can also be something. For the first time the concept of Zen started making sense.

I don't know where the boat appeared from or whether it had been in the bay all along, but I only noticed it after a while. I was in such a Zen mode that it didn't even appear suspicious that a boat would drop anchor in a bay without a harbour. It was not your usual tourist boat that takes people for diving lessons, but I only realised this afterwards. After my shoot with Pauli, I did not register much.

Shortly after that a second boat appeared and cast anchor next to the first one. Goods were loaded onto the first boat. I was convinced that all the pirates had died, but piracy was obviously still alive and well and it hit me that we were witnessing an illegal transaction. Pauli and I discussed what was going on but we did not think that our presence could be a problem to the people on the boats. It was like watching a movie or seeing how guys catch crayfish out of season on the West Coast. Sure, it was illegal, but like stealing fruit in your neighbour's orchard as a child, it was naughty rather than criminal.

The next moment a guy appeared behind us. He wore khaki pants, issued an aggressive growl and wielded a panga. His vibe was definitely not Zen. He wanted to know who we were, what we were doing there and what we had seen. He wasn't nearly as eloquent as

Captain Jack Sparrow, but we quickly convinced him that we were there by pure chance. When he asked where we were staying, we lied about the hotel's name.

Pauli immediately collected our stuff and told him that we were on our way. The panga man thought this was a good idea. He also encouraged us to forget everything we saw and not to mention it to anyone. We were quick to assure him that we couldn't agree more.

Île Sainte-Marie continued to surprise us. An even more surrealistic experience awaited us, but we would first get to know the island people better.

On the music scene not much was going on. The live music lacked originality and the music you heard in bars and restaurants was mostly by foreign artists. Lucky Dube's face decorated many a bar wall, although some depictions were more lifelike than others. The CDs were often pirate copies, but you could still get Eddie Grant's music on the island.

We also noticed that most island inhabitants did not have a burning desire to know what was going on in their own country or the rest of the world. There was no radio station or television. The goings on in front of their houses seemed to be sufficient. Newspapers didn't reach the island for days and then it was much more in demand as wallpaper than reading matter.

On a cultural front, Rambo stole the show. Pirate copies of all Sylvester Stallone's movies survived a four hour long boat trip by entrepreneurs wishing to spread the Gospel of Violence. In most cases they were fourth or fifth generation copies with Chinese subtitles. The only exception was *The Italion Stallion*, the porno flick he made before he became famous. That one never made it to the island.

Rambo roared from "movie theatres" everywhere, which were wooden huts on poles equipped with a television screen, video machine and small pews arranged in front of the TV. The entry fee was the equivalent of 15c. Even though the door and window openings were covered with pieces of cloth, it was sweltering inside. The hut was usually crowded with children and men drinking beer.

Every time Rambo killed off a baddy, there was great cheering and stamping of feet. The video was often stopped and rewound to watch the scene again. Some of the children wore red headbands and used sticks as guns. During the boring bits with lots of dialogue and too little action, the children escaped to practice action scenes outside.

Rambo has had a marked influence on large parts of the continent. In my opinion most wars in Africa since the nineties were started by children fed on a Rambo flick diet. In the wars in the Democratic Republic of the Congo, Liberia and in Sierra Leone there was always more than one commander-in-chief who used the *nom de guerre* Rambo.

If a revolution ever breaks out on Île Sainte-Marie, I bet you five Three Horses the commander's name will be Rambo and he will sport a red headband. In time he'll issue an order that he is the only person allowed to carry the name and wear the headband. This, of course, will lead to his eventual assassination.

Fortunately, chances are slim that there will ever be a revolution on Île Sainte-Marie, because they are a gentle people. This is most probably where Hollywood's script writers got the idea of island living where everything happens at a snail's pace and no one is ever bothered by anything. Our doors didn't have any locks and most of the time the only police station on the island was unmanned. One day we saw the police chief in a bar. He was in the company of a fat Belgium surrounded by extremely willing island maidens. Like any tropical police chief worth his salt he wore his hat at a jaunty angle and his uniform shirt was unbuttoned. Did he do something right, or did he screw up to get this job, I had to wonder.

Discounting Three Horses, another popular drink on the island was litchi rum. Locals made it in big ten litre bottles and left the litchis in the brew. When you ordered a tot, it always came with a litchi. Now two tots of litchi rum put you in a really mellow mood. After three it always seems much later than it really is, and after four you pine for your bed. Five or six will erase your memory of the whole evening and after seven you'll do the things you read about in *Heat*. But strangely enough one never sees drunken people on the island.

I can't remember exactly when we met the Three Musketeers aka the Horny Frenchmen. When I think about it they seemed to have been there all the time. We visited the island out of season[4] and they were the only other guests in the dining room. It was inevitable that we would strike up a conversation.

The Horny Frenchmen were busy building a wooden house for a rich French industrialist. The architect worked out the dimensions of the house in feet, but for some reason these bright sparks thought the plans were in metres. This minor mistake had interesting results. It was as though one was looking at the house through a looking-glass. Everything was in proportion, but just so much larger than usual. The doors were twice the normal dimensions, the ceiling was high enough to accommodate a jumping basketball player and the veranda had an echo. By the time they realised their mistake, it was too late and they muddled through. A project that should have lasted three weeks eventually took three months to complete.

When we met them, the Horny Frenchmen's funds were nearly depleted and to save money they lived in the half-finished house. The

---

4   August is high season in Madagascar, because tourists come from all corners of the world to watch the whales mate. Or as some put it so eloquently: "When the humpback whales come to hump."

little money they had left was spent on irregular meals in the hotel and litres of litchi rum. The three handsome French boys (Pauli's words, not mine) were either not interested in, or didn't have the money to entertain the local ladies. They targeted my wife.

There is truth to the rumour that a tropical island reveals a woman's natural sensuality. This could very well be one of the reasons why Mauritius is such a popular honeymoon destination for South Africans. By this time Pauli looked like a sun-kissed goddess, extremely comfortable in her own skin. Because of the heat she didn't wear much. I could barely contain myself.

If I were a different person, Thierry, Flo and Bruno (as they were more commonly known) could have been the victims of the standard South African machismo. But since Pauli clearly enjoyed the attention and as I trusted her implicitly, we decided that the Three Musketeers could continue with their game.

It seemed that they drew lots to determine the order in which they would try their luck with Pauli. To get to Pauli, they first had to get around me, of course. First they brought me copious amounts of booze in the hope of getting me so drunk that I would pass out, but they had no idea who they were up against. Then they followed a more subtle approach by offering us dagga, which would supposedly break down one's resistance. That didn't work either.

Next they tried the oldest trick in the book when two of them asked me to join them for an outing, while the third accidentally bumped into Pauli on the beach. They were still unsuccessful. Bruno was the keenest of the three or perhaps he had a point to prove. Later Thierry even followed us to Tana to check that Pauli hadn't changed her mind. The game continued for days and Pauli and I had a good laugh at all their antics.

So, there I had it – all the excitement I was looking for, maybe even a bit too much. It's the strangest feeling when you see other men trying to seduce your wife. On the one hand you are flattered that someone desires something of yours, but on the other hand it is a true test for your relationship. In the end, I knew that it was up to her who she wanted to have sex with, irrespective of what I said or did.

The hotel arranged a special Christmas Eve dinner and the Horny Frenchmen knew that this would be their last chance to make a move on Pauli. We would be flying back to Tana the day after Christmas. Our French phrase book, which contained handy questions like "where is the metro?" and "how much for this champagne?", also taught me how to wish someone merry Christmas in French: "Joyeux Noel!" Many women, including Pauli, are impressed by a French accent, and I therefore began to study the booklet in earnest.

I had also hoped that I would recognise a French word or two if the Horny Frenchmen discussed us while they were in our company. Our hotel's small library was hardly adequate and mostly contained books left behind by other travellers, and fortunately no Afrikaans-French dictionaries. My phrase book knowledge and Pauli's high school French, of which they were not aware, convinced me that we would have the upper hand. I, or rather we, were ready for the final onslaught.

That evening Pauli's transparent cotton dress showcased her bronze body to perfection. The flowers on the dress only covered the bare essentials and left very little to the imagination. We were six people – the two of us, the Horny Frenchmen and Sonia, the beautiful hotel representative. The Three Musketeers probably convinced Sonia to join us thinking that another woman in the group would help to put Pauli at ease. Then again, Sonia might have sensed the sexual tension and was perhaps intrigued by it. Either way, that night she let her professional guard down and partied as if she were part of the plot.

The meal was memorable, but by this time we were so used to good food that it didn't take us long to consume the three course meal. Everyone seemed keen to get the meal out of the way. Bruno

regaled us with his experiences at a New York sex club. He tried to
fish whether we swing.

After dinner the Horny Frenchmen suggested that we play poker
and suggested that anyone who lost a round should down a shot of
litchi rum. It was a bad idea, because you were bound to vomit and
Pauli was not into shooters. She suggested strip poker instead and as
expected the Horny Frenchmen were all for it. Bruno was the first
to lose all his clothes and wasn't shy to show off his assets.

The thing about straight men is that they never know exactly
how well (or poorly) endowed they are. Their frame of reference
is limited to their own dad (whom they last saw naked as a child
when everything and everyone is bigger in comparison to you) and
the women with whom they have had sex. Women, wily as they are,
will almost always say that you're large, even if you are the size of
an acorn. So their opinions are not to be trusted.

I could understand Bruno's confidence, but Thierry and Flo
crossed their legs like girls. Sonia had breasts a plastic surgeon could
use to advertise his handiwork even though she had not been near
one. And for some reason I won so many rounds that I remained
almost fully clothed right up until the end.

After our last game, Pauli did not have a stitch of clothing left.
She got up and casually walked out of the restaurant. All you could
see was the tan lines on her firm bottom. She didn't look back once.
The Horny Frenchmen gaped like fish on dry ground. Clearly their
crossed legs were a preventive measure. Pauli knew what impression she left. Later while I enjoyed a smoke with the three of them
on the beach and Sonia had gone to sleep, Flo told me how much
he liked Pauli.

When I got into bed, next to my beautiful wife whose body was
bathed in moonlight, she was still awake. I told her that Flo was
smitten with her. "I prefer Bruno," was all she said.

I decided to leave it at that.

One evening back in Tana she grew quite melancholy after a few glasses of wine and told me: "Once in my life I have to have a French lover."

Arghhh. Women – can't live with them, can't kill them.

During our week on the island, Pauli developed a strong bond with the children of the small local town. When the young girls went for a swim, she joined them and they tried to teach each other their language with gestures.

Every time the hotel security guard chased them away from the beach and told them not to disturb the rich, white holiday-makers, Pauli scolded him and invited the children back. Even though they could not understand her, they listened to Pauli's every word, because they could sense her sincere interest.

The island's inhabitants were dirt poor. They caught fish and planted crops to survive. If the storm destroyed your crops, your family had to go hungry until the next season. When a tropical storm blew away their roofs, their only option was to go out and pick more banana leaves to repair it. The children seldom had enough stationery for school; their parents simply could not afford it. And if by chance they had the money, the stationery was not necessarily available.

That was why Pauli decided that all the children should get a small Christmas present of sweets and a pen. We brought 100 *stilos* and 200 *bon-bons* and asked the security guard to tell the children to come round on Christmas morning. Our escapades from the previous evening were long forgotten by the time the children arrived. They did not know the Santa Clause fable and none of them had a Christmas tree at home or had ever received a Christmas present.

The children got into a row of their own accord and Pauli gave each of them a pen and two sweets. To prevent them from slipping into the line again, I painted the nail of their little fingers with Pauli's nail varnish. Two of them chanced it, but I recognised them even though their nails were clean after they had scrubbed it with sea sand. The security guard was surprised that I had recognised them. He grabbed them by the ears and removed them while the rest of the gang cheered loudly.

Our account for a week's drinks, three course meals of duck l'orange and crayfish amounted to nearly R1 500. The *maître d'* got a ten percent tip. He nearly slapped a slobbery kiss on my mouth. It was more than his monthly salary.

Pauli's part of the holiday was over and it was time to move on to Antananarivo for part two. Sonia wasn't there to wish us everything of the best. She was either recovering from her hangover or she couldn't face us.

Our flight from Ambodifotatra back to Antananarivo on the main island should not take up more than a sentence in this story. But our twin-engined aeroplane was built in 1949, a year after the National Party came into power and we all know what happened to them. A cyclone was closing in on Île Sainte-Marie and it did not bode well for our flight.

I believe pigeons are as comfortable in free flight as a human is driving a car. Of course, people are not meant to be in the air and pigeons should not be moving about on the roads. That is why so many pigeons become road kill. I am also a firm believer in fate, even though my chemist at the Linden Pharmacy believes that I have to be at peace with God to truly understand it, but that is a story for another time.

Each time the 1949 dinky aeroplane was caught in storm clouds and air currents the air pocket caused a sudden loss of height. Due to a lack of resistance the propellers made a high-pitched whining noise, as if the plane were falling from the sky. I lay down on the floor of the plane and tried to meditate. When that did not work, I called on a Higher Being for the first time in decades. I was really scared this time.

When we landed in Tana, I fell down on my knees and kissed the tarmac. I was so focussed on my own survival that I did not even check whether Pauli got off the plane safely. Till this day I don't know whether the flight took ten or sixty minutes.

Reliable Kenny, the tour guide who first welcomed us in Tana, met us at the airport again and took us to the Hotel Tana Plaza. We booked this three star tourist trap because their website indicated that they had a lobby. As we are huge fans of lobbies we simply had to stay there. They also proudly announced that the bed linen was part of the service and included in the price of the hotel room.

The Hotel Tana Plaza was supposed to have satellite television, but their website failed to mention that all seven channels broadcasted in French only. After a week without any access to news reports, the journalist in me was dying for an update but the *coup d'état* in the Ivory Coast was only happening in French. At least it was more exciting than the programme on the local channel showing people how to make charcoal. By the end of the show you realise that the technique they have just taught you is completely useless and that charcoal is nothing but brittle flakes. Even so, they aired the programme.

Since the view from our room was even less thrilling (it looked out onto a backyard where someone was busy force-feeding ducks for foie gras), we decided to go and explore Tana straight away. The city looked like the set for a gangster movie in the tropics and I expected Pierce Brosnan to come walking around the next corner, donning a fedora.

But on this particular Sunday afternoon the streets were deserted. There was no one in sight, except the guy who tried to rob us. First he begged for some money, but to no avail. Then he invaded my personal space as he tried to get his hand into my pocket to snatch my wallet. When that also didn't work, he threatened and intimidated us. What made the situation so ludicrous was the fact that he was unarmed. After I pushed him away forcefully, he casually walked back to his corner where he resumed his siesta.

After a week of peaceful relaxation the attempted robbery came as quite a shock. We returned to the hotel immediately and had an afternoon nap to recover from the previous two nights on Île Sainte-Marie. When we woke up, we had regained some of our courage and decided to brave Tana's streets again. We are not scared away that easily and by now we had built up a reputation as intrepid travellers after all.

After the siesta Tana was an entirely different city and the streets swarmed with people. During the next week I found out that siestas are an integral part of the Madagascan economy. On Mondays people worked half day and only ran their most important errands. Tuesdays and Wednesdays were full working days Madagascan style, which meant that all the shops and offices were closed between twelve and three. Thursday was wedding day and the city was crowded with brides and their grooms. No one worked and even the traffic came to a screeching halt. On Fridays they made the necessary preparations for the weekend. It slowly dawned on me why most of them only earned R150 a month.

When we left the hotel that evening, my first thought was that I was in the wrong movie because there were Father Christmases everywhere. The night market was on and several black men in woolly red suits with stick-on white beards had their own Father Christmas stall. Each stall was decorated slightly differently and children could choose who they wanted to be photographed with. They were all dressed up in their finery and queued to have their picture taken.

There's a marked Eastern influence in Madagascan clothing. There were lots of shiny details and imitation silk, gold trimmings and ruffles. A strict caste system applies in the society: the darker your skin colour, the likelier you are to be regarded as a hillbilly. The more Eastern your features, the greater your chances of getting a good job and making something of your life. But all the colourful outfits could not conceal the hundreds of street children and beggars, many of whom had polio or were disabled. In the quiet, romantic main street of a few hours ago, rich shades and abject poverty now blended into a farcical scene.

You could buy almost anything on the street and I got myself a neatly pressed *Time* for R25. It was only a week old. A day or so later I found an English book about Saddam Hussein in a bookshop that was imported from Canada. The person who ordered it probably thought it would be in French. Pauli and I timed each other to make sure that one of us did not spend a second more with the book than the other.

The highlight of our day was when we discovered Patisserie Colbert where real espresso and puff pastries containing small pieces of chocolate were served by waiters with white cloths over their forearms. To top it off it was so cheap that we could settle our bill with small change. Good espresso and puff pastry weren't limited to Tana alone. When we stopped at a garage some way out of the city later that week, the truck drivers stood in queues at the small shops selling these excellent French exports.[5]

We spent Sunday night in our hotel room surfing through all the French satellite channels until we found *The Horse Whisperer,* which was broadcast in English with French subtitles. Not even the fact that it was the only thing we could watch made it more interesting.

Fortunately it was the last evening we would spend in our hotel room. The next morning we found out that Tana broke all African records with the number of parties held there. We would start each

---

5   Pauli eventually found the only decent toilet in a brothel. The owner very subtly closed the doors of the rooms where prostitutes already waited for their clients.

evening with a meal of epic proportions. Not only the French left their mark on the Madagascan cuisine, but so did the Chinese, Indians and Arabs. Dinner with foie gras as a starter and crayfish as main course accompanied by a good bottle of KWV would set us back a measly R150. That included a cognac and cigar for both of us – and that was only because the Americans had not yet discovered Madagascar.

On Monday morning I started my mission to find the legendary Madagascan guitar player Etienne "Bouboul" Ramboatiana. One of Madagascar's greatest contributions to the world is its guitar players. The unique style of contemporary guitar players like Eric Manana and D'Gary has charmed people across the world, but it is the now forgotten heroes who laid the foundation for their success. Bouboul was one of them.

In Madagascar you hear music everywhere. It either blares from scratchy loudspeakers on the verge of giving in or you hear it live on the streets. In any dusty hamlet you'll find a group of musicians getting a party started. The equipment and musicians may have seen better days, but the music was top quality. In Madagascar people don't even need liquor to have a good party.

Bouboul was introduced to the world in the sixties by an American circus owner who heard him play in a bar in Tana. He started performing with the circus in Maputo (then Lourenço Marques), went to Mombassa and then criss-crossed the world with his background music for circus animals. Most people have forgotten Bouboul, but music fundis and Madagascan guitar players regard him as a god. I had previously read about him on Ian Anderson's Rootsworld website and was determined to meet him while I was there.

With Kenny's help it was unexpectedly easy to track down Bouboul. He of course got a decent tip for his trouble. Kenny soon became our negotiator and took us to places not normally frequented by tourists. To supplement his measly salary he started spending more time with us than he did at the travel agency.

He also started dressing differently. On our first day at the airport he wore a neat shirt, pants and a tie. He was now wearing shorts, sandals and an unbuttoned shirt. As he started to relax in our company, he would drink a beer with me and told us many stories about the real Madagascar. His stories were filled with pathos. He knew that there was a world outside of Madagascar, but he didn't know how to become part of it. Kenny became a tour guide in the hope that it would enable him to get out of the country. In every African country I have ever visited I've met at least ten Kennys, but sadly for most of them it will remain a dream to escape from their circumstances.

Kenny's uncle had a taxi and he offered to take me to Bouboul at a discounted fee. In Tana all taxis are Renaults. Your success as a taxi owner is measured against the age of your car with the newest taxis about ten years old. Kenny's uncle drove a Renault 4, which was manufactured between 1961 and 1994. His taxi was definitely one of the first models and in Europe it would have been a treasured museum piece. In Tana it was a means of survival.

The interior of the Renault was stripped of any luxuries such as seats or a starter. The backseat was a rickety wooden bench, smartly decorated with a crocheted pillow – an ingenious safety feature that protected your coccyx from serious injury. The door was securely fastened by a sliding bolt usually seen in the toilets of bars. The door panels were removed and there were no windows apart from the windscreen. A handle was attached to the inside of the roof and was very handy to hang on to for dear life.

When I enquired about the missing starter, Kenny reassured me that there was no problem. He showed me the piece of wire that was attached to the starter motor and which had to be pulled like a lawn mower to start the engine. Despite these unique features the car boasted a fresh coat of blue paint and the interior and exterior were spotless.

Bouboul lived in the outskirts of Tana. Near his house we encountered a hill that was way too steep for the Renault. We had to get out and push it up the hill with the aid of a few helpers. In view of the fact that everything that goes up has to come down, I recommended that we leave the taxi at the top of the hill and walk the last five minutes to Bouboul's house. Kenny and his uncle accepted the suggestion enthusiastically.

I'm not sure what I expected, but Bouboul's house looked like all the others in the washed-out neighbourhood. Even though the island had much more space than the average European city, the French imported their architecture to Madagascar without changing a thing. Consequently, you'd find narrow three-storey buildings in the middle of huge stands. Bouboul's house was as narrow as it was high.

He was fairly tiny and a short old man, but he still had a glint in his eyes. After he stopped touring in the mid-seventies, he began to record Madagascar's music history and taught young people to play guitar in true island style. He took in all-comers, whether they could pay or not.

His home was scantily furnished with old, but well cared for furniture. He sat in an upright wooden chair and explained the various guitar styles to me for 90 minutes. I couldn't speak French and he was not fluent in English, but thanks to Kenny and the sounds of his guitar I left as a friend. I could see that he was not well-off and offered to pay him for his time, but he refused my offer with a smile.

On the way back to the car, Kenny translated his last words. "He said you should rather write something about him."

I always keep my promises.

We drove back to the hotel through Tana's slums against the setting sun. I couldn't believe my luck. I had met a living legend.

In the following days we had dinner in a restaurant where we were served a whole, grilled duck, head still attached. It watched with a beady eye as we consumed him piece by piece. This is what happens when you eat in restaurants where the menus are only in French or Chinese. Then there was the incident with the ATM that only had digits on its keyboard and no letters. Minor problem there since I always remember my PIN as a word and not as a number and we urgently needed money.

In between all of this, we also had to decide what we wanted to do on New Year's Eve. It was the end of a millennium and either the world would go up in flames or we would wake up stranded on a tropical island in a post-apocalyptic era. Whichever happened, I felt it called for a do or die party. Not that we were not already partying every night, but that evening we wanted to do something special.

I saw a poster advertising a New Year's Eve party, but Kenny first had to translate it for me before I knew what it was all about. It transpired that the government was organising a big concert in Tana's soccer stadium where Madagascar's most popular musicians would perform. And best of all, the concert was free.

By this time we had already looted the credit card twice. If you earn a salary, January is always a difficult month with many expenses. Unless the world stopped turning the children would need school-books and uniforms, so free entertainment sounded like the perfect option. Kenny tried hard to dissuade us, saying that it would be too dangerous with all the drunken and criminal elements in the audience. Tourists are generally advised not to be out on the streets after dark and we more or less kept to that rule. But after the exceptionally amateurish effort to rob us and the fact that we knew the city pretty well by then, I thought we should be able to manage it.

When Kenny's uncle heard we were planning an outing he was extremely disappointed that we weren't making use of his services. Since the trip would involve night-time driving and as his Renault didn't have any headlights, I decided not to take any chances. One should not tempt fate.

The Mahamsina Municipal Stadium is the home of the national soccer team. The Barea, as the national team is called, had never qualified for any major tournament. This might be because Barea is a kind of cow ("zebu") and cows aren't exactly known for their soccer skills. Madagascar's soccer bosses might learn a thing or two from Nigeria's Super Eagles, Zambia's Copper Bullets or Senegal's Lions of Teranga.

The stadium could accommodate 30 000 people, but it didn't have a single toilet. Everyone did their business in the grass around the stadium, so you had to watch your step.

What Kenny failed to mention was that seeing that the government was footing the bill, they would get their pound of flesh. A variety of VIPs each got a chance to address the audience in Malagasy. The president might have been there, but I hadn't had time to memorise his long name. The crowd was only half interested. They took their drinking much more seriously. Everyone waited for the party to start.

When the music eventually started, it was soon evident that the more commercial Madagascan groups were going to perform at the concert, supported by dancers in uniforms who performed synchronized dance moves. Commercial music – in any language – has never been my thing. There were too many keyboards and too few percussionists. It was worlds apart from the down and dirty music we had heard during the last few days. The rest of the crowd did not share my lack of enthusiasm.

When the third or fourth group took to the stage, I noticed that as Pauli and I moved around in the stadium a growing number of people started to follow us. At first only a small group was interested in us, but as the people got drunker more of them came up to us and offered us liquor.

This was the very liquor I had tried to avoid like the plague the entire week – bottles of locally brewed gin or whisky at R20 a pop. Before our departure, I had a hepatitis injection and an extra polio shot for good measure on the recommendation of the German travel doctor in Johannesburg. I was willing to share a joint with a stranger, but there I drew the line. I was pretty sure my injections weren't potent enough to protect me against an array of bugs if I shared a bottle with a whole group of people.

As the night progressed and the liquor gave our companions Dutch courage, the friendly offers began to sound more and more like instructions. The bottles of liquor were passed on with an attitude of "you *will* take a swig". After some time I looked around us and realised that we were the only white souls in the crowd. We had become a bigger attraction than the groups on the stage. Within minutes we were engulfed by different groups of people who wanted to be our close personal friends and tell us their drunken tales in Malagasy.

I wouldn't exactly say that I panicked or that I felt threatened, but my personal space was definitely invaded like never before. The last straw was when the different groups started fighting with each other for our attention. I was afraid that the situation could become extremely unpleasant. It did not help that the music sucked. It was time to go.

Outside the stadium a single taxi was waiting patiently – the same one that had brought us to it. I could only admire the driver for his common sense: what goes in must come out. He just smiled when we got in.

The only problem was that it wasn't midnight yet and we had very little time to find another party. At the taxi driver's recommendation we went to a club a stone's throw away from our hotel. Somehow we had not been there before. The R20 entrance fee included a handmade hat. The inside of the club was brimming with Christmas decorations and the group on stage alternated their own compositions with Michael Jackson covers. Even though I don't like his music I, like anyone with a basic knowledge of music, know that only Michael can do Michael. Sadly someone forgot to mention this to the band.

When Pauli went to the loo, the bouncer offered me the services of various girls at R30 apiece. Some of them were quite pretty and he couldn't understand why I wasn't interested. But by now I had given up trying to explain my story to people who could not understand English.

It was an excellent party and I danced like a mad man. When we fell into the airport bus at four o'clock the next morning, I did feel as though doomsday was upon us. At the airport a customs official threatened me for trying to take a walking stick made of protected wood out of the country, but he really wanted my boarding pass to buy duty free whisky. My energy levels were at an all time low. I did not even put up a fight.

At the airport back in Johannesburg our welcoming committee consisted of a few cleaners and a listless immigration official who stamped our passports in slow motion. No one searched our baggage.

It was obvious we were not the only ones who had partied as if tomorrow would never come.

# THE FIVE NATIONS TOUR
## Destination Malawi, 2000

LET ME START by saying it was all Pauli's idea. Usually the best ones are, but this was not her brightest moment.

In theory the plan was quite simple. Our boys, who were young teenagers then, spent most of their time in shopping malls where they watched American movies and hung out with their affluent, white school friends. Pauli felt they were growing up under too much Western influence and that they didn't have a clue what living on our continent really meant.

We wanted to show them Africa. Not the Africa that you can do from the safety of your air-conditioned 4x4, but the real deal where you kick back with the locals, buy your food in the market and sleep on the floor of a mission station. The true Africa, the one they are living in without even being fully aware of it.

Pauli and I don't have children together, but I have two boys from a previous marriage, Gerrad and Axl, and Marnu is Pauli's son from a previous marriage. The three boys had just become adolescents and the age difference between the eldest and youngest was only three years. While Gerrad was the eldest, Marnu was the biggest of the three. Also, Marnu stayed with us, while my two sons lived with their mother in Phalaborwa. Anyone who has teenagers will know that this combination was a recipe for trouble and the inevitable power struggles.

The boys would be spending fourteen days on the backseat of a Mercedes for a distance of 6 420 kilometres. The plan was to drive through Botswana and Zambia to Malawi where we would take a few days to relax at the lake. To finish our "Five Nations tour" we would return via Mozambique and Zimbabwe. We had no idea where we would stay, thinking we'd sort things out as we got there. Lastly, my scant knowledge of towing a trailer didn't prevent me from getting one – another thing that would have to be figured out along the way.

Have I mentioned that I'm not the camping type, and also that I'm not a very practical person? Our previous camping expedition in Mozambique went horribly wrong and we had to sit in the car for half a day as our little tent was blown away by a violent hurricane. So there would be no camping on this trip. My only concession with regard to planning was to hide two jerry cans of petrol in the trailer and enough pen-light batteries to keep the children's Nintendo's going. I would far rather have run out of petrol than be without batteries.

Of course, it's very different travelling by road than it is to fly to a country. When you fly to an African country you are only hassled by customs officials once. You give him (or her) a few dollars and that's the end of it. But when you're on the road, you are subject to the power games of every single person that wears a uniform. The branch in the middle of the road didn't just miraculously appear. It was put there on purpose so that you could be legally stolen from. When you stop, the guy manning the "roadblock" will slowly come walking up to your car while he stretches like a tiger ready to pounce. When he sees the Mercedes and its lily-white occupants, he'll struggle to hide his big smile. He has just hit the jackpot and maybe he'll get lucky with the cute girl he has been eyeing because tonight he'll have a few dollars to spend on her.

In theory I don't have a problem with this system because I have always supported the small businessman regardless of the guise in which he appears. The fact of the matter is that the official in question has probably not received his salary for a couple of months because the government has run out of money or it was stolen by his boss. And even if he did receive his salary, chances are slim that it will be enough for any kind of social life. Surely in such circumstances a young man should be allowed to earn some money with his AK47 with which to enjoy life before he becomes old and cynical like the rest of us. He might be thirsty, long for a cigarette or need the money to pay for his children's school fund. As it was just before Christmas, I knew I would be expected to make several such contributions along the way and to this day I believe that my open wallet made many children very happy on Christmas morning.

Of course, in practice things aren't necessarily as simple as this. Instead of telling you straight out how much it will cost to remove the big branch from the road so that you can get on your way, there always has to be a protracted negotiation process. First you are ordered out of the car. Then the official wants to know where you are coming from and where you are going. While we talk, we walk around the car, and he kicks the tyres to determine whether they are in good order. Then I have to explain who is related to whom in the car while he scratches about in the trailer that I had to open. Only then do the negotiations start.

If you're lucky, he'll name his price while you are standing by the car. Then the conversation usually goes as follows:

"I am very hungry; do you have $10 for some food for me?"

"Sorry my brother, as you can see I have a car full of children that I have to feed. How about a cigarette?"

"Ok, that is very kind of you, sir. Enjoy your journey."

But it can also go the other, slightly more expensive way. In that instance you are invited to the shady tree where a more senior officer awaits you with a warm smile. The conversation then goes as follows:

"We are very hungry; do you have $20 for some food for us?"

"Sorry my brother, as you can see I have a car full of children that I have to feed. How about a packet of cigarettes?"

"Ok, that is very kind of you, sir. Enjoy your journey."

Unfortunately this technique didn't work in the Tete corridor in Mozambique, but I'll get to that later.

There are two reasons why one should not travel around Africa in a Mercedes, even if it's an old, second-hand model. Firstly, you will always cough up more at roadblocks even if the other cars are more expensive than yours. A Mercedes, irrespective of its age, implies that you have money or at least had money at some point. Secondly, the Mercedes has a reasonably advanced suspension system. The trailer that we borrowed from friends was like a sardine tin with Marie biscuit wheels. When we hit a pothole the Merc could handle it, but not the trailer. These were all things I would learn during our trip.

Oh, and another thing to keep in mind when travelling through southern Africa by road are the taxes you will be required to pay at every border. In each country you have to pay to get access to the exclusive club of road users for that country. Of course the worse the roads and the more corrupt the country, the more expensive your membership. This I would also learn later.

We entered Botswana through a border post called Platjan for a mere pittance: R12 (R8 for third party cover and R4 for insurance). The pole that blocked the road was rusty and the caravan that served as the office and accommodation was worn with age. Every single one of the five people who went through that border post during the past ten years will tell you that the customs officials are so surprised to see you that they don't even think of exploiting you. They clearly had enough cigarettes and beverages. It takes exactly ten minutes to get out of South Africa and into Botswana. This was the official start of our Five Nations tour. Up until then the children had argued only once and the Nintendo batteries were still going strong.

The rule was that the children were only allowed to play Nintendo when we were on the open road. Once we entered a town they had to switch it off and take in the surroundings. Sometimes there was a difference of opinion about what qualified as a town. At their tender age they already knew quite a bit about their democratic rights and as the three of them often outvoted me and Pauli I had to insist on presidential privilege. Later on in the trip I had to declare the car an autocracy to settle disagreements quickly.

Luckily it was no problem to convince them to stop playing Nintendo when we reached roadblocks. They were so scared of losing their games during the negotiations that they quickly pushed them under their bums and smiled angelically at the man with the gun. Their smiles assured me that the huge account for their orthodontic treatment was all worth it.

Botswana could very well be the Switzerland of Africa if only it weren't for the death sentence they mete out so generously. It's regarded as the most stable democracy in the region, but I guess that's only because there are not enough people to cause serious problems. The fine dust from the dirt road between Platjan and Francistown, as well as the trees along the road meant that we would not have been able to see any people, even if there were any. But at least it wasn't as lonely a journey as driving through Namibia where you often travel in a straight line towards the horizon for up to two hours.

Francistown is one of the oldest towns in Botswana and few people know that southern Africa's first gold rush took place here (in 1867 to be exact and thanks to a guy named Karl Mauch). I'm sure the town is brimming with stories, but all one sees are cheap Chinese shops and shopping malls in South African style. Francistown looks like your average South African platteland town where the council is still maintaining the sewerage system and the mayor and his friends have not spent all the money on official cars. If I wanted to sell this as the true Africa to the boys I should have left them in Phalaborwa.

Still, to soften the culture shock their first lunch outside of South

Africa was at Steers. Francistown was not the kind of place I wanted to stay in too long, so after lunch we headed to Zambia. That night we slept in rustic rondavels just before the Zambian border and I tried to wash down the day's dust with one of Africa's most tasteless beers, St Louis. The beer captured the character of Botswana pretty well.

Colonialism is often portrayed as if it had a uniform effect on all African countries, but this is not necessarily the case. Each of the colonial authorities did their thing in their own way. The English's special contribution to our continent was to strip local inhabitants of their culture. So much so that the former English colonies like Botswana (and Zambia, as I was soon to find out) were some of the most boring places I have ever visited. These two countries have about as much character as a fresh banana peel. It's as if the locals can't remember who they really are. You taste it in their beer, see it in their clothes and definitely hear it in their music. If you don't believe me, name one pop group from these two countries that made it internationally.

Zimbabwe is the exception and I don't include South Africa, because we weren't under English rule long enough for them to steal our culture. In any event we are such mavericks that they wouldn't have succeeded even if they tried. They did succeed in lousing up our beer, which I rank the most boring in the world.

We did experience some excitement when we nearly collided with an elephant on the highway. The car in front of me braked sharply and immediate reversed to get away from the charging elephant. I have never tried to reverse with a trailer and soon realised it's an art all its own, especially when an ear-flapping elephant crosses your path.

In Botswana's defense I have to say that it was the first country in Africa where no one was interested in being paid in American dollars. The pula was too strong and therefore nobody needed the dollars. There was also a complete lack of roadblocks and no one expected a gift from me. That was rather decent of them, I thought.

If you want to see chaos at its most organised, Kazangulu is a good place to start. This is where you have to cross the Zambezi River to go into Zambia. However, there is a dispute between Botswana, Zambia and Zimbabwe over this area and that's why there isn't a bridge across the river. The stand-off has been dragging on for years.

Unfortunately, the maintenance money for the ferry was spent elsewhere and rows of heavily laden trucks waited their turn on the floating piece of plank with its smoking diesel engine. No effort was made to balance the ferry during loading and the one side was nearly under water while the other side lifted up in the air. The river teemed with hippopotamus and seemingly listless crocodiles baked in the sun. I know they were waiting for the ferry to overturn. A few weeks after we crossed the river, the ferry did overturn. Nineteen passengers were allegedly eaten by crocodiles.

The usual chaos to get a spot on the ferry is aggravated by the hundreds of people who want to make a few cents out of you by acting as your guide. Fact is, if you don't jump the queue you'll wait for days. Some of the truck drivers, who are under pressure to get their loads to its destination as soon as possible, jump the queue and don't hesitate to threaten you. It's either that or they were just plain rude.

What did happen was that the children suddenly stopped fighting. They stared at the pandemonium around them with wide eyes. The Nintendos were forgotten. When it was necessary they communicated properly with the local shysters and even showed some empathy for my shattered nerves. They kindly offered to organise me a cool drink, although they would have had to walk back to Francistown to get it. I think it's safe to say that this experience shook them up a little. Johannesburg's malls were forgotten. At last they were experiencing a piece of the real Africa. Although they looked like deer caught in the headlights, I must say I felt very proud.

After a great deal of difficulty, a seemingly endless wait and several rounds of negotiations we eventually got room on the ferry. We were blissfully unaware of what awaited us.

On the other side of the Zambezi the chief customs official at the Zambian border post decided our Mercedes was stolen and he blankly refused us entry into the country. The certified duplicate documents that confirmed my ownership meant nothing to him. I coaxed, pleaded and eventually offered him a bribe. When he refused the bribe, I knew we were in deep trouble.

At that stage the children started to freak out. They didn't go off the rails entirely, but I could see that the situation unnerved them. I tried to calm them down by saying that I had enough money to buy us out of any kind of accusation, including a murder charge.

The customs official would not budge. Later somebody told me that a large car theft syndicate had been bust at the border post the previous week and that white South Africans were involved. Various customs officials were fired because of their involvement. In the customs official's expert opinion we had to drive back to Johannesburg and bring the original papers. Only then would he let us through.

We had lost all hope when Pauli came to our rescue with one of her ingenious plans. She waited until the official went on lunch and approached a female customs official. A few minutes later she walked towards us with a huge smile and stamped documents. By that time the children's energy was flagging in the relentless African sun but they quickly leapt into the car and we headed straight for the gate. In front of us an official and a motorist were involved in a loud argument – they caught him smuggling petrol into the country. This is a very serious offence in Zambia where petrol costs three times more than in Botswana. When the motorist was arrested and taken away, I suddenly remembered the two jerry cans in the trailer. My blood turned cold. I certainly didn't want to get into more trouble just because I brought two cans of unleaded petrol as an emergency back up measure.

Luckily the customs official was so involved in the arrest that we could easily slip through. As the gate was slowly beginning to open for us, I saw in my rear-view mirror the chief customs official storming out of the building. He headed straight for us, but I put my foot down and sped off. It was time to have lunch in Livingstone.

Entry fee to Club Zambia: $20 for the ferry, $20 for third party cover, $15 for insurance and a fine of R64 for something I can't even remember. This excluded a waiting period of two and a half hours. I instinctively knew the roads were going to be very bad.

In Livingstone we went to the Victoria Falls and ended up having a meal with a trendy Scotsman with a broken jaw. Weird how one remembers such trivial things.

The road from Livingstone to Lusaka was under construction and the entire stretch of 600 kilometres was a muddy mess. We had to brave the dirt road with a convoy of trucks while the rain came down in buckets. The slipping and sliding would have been amusing if it wasn't so frustrating. My remark to the boys that this was bundu bashing at its best only brought grunted replies. The journey was taking much longer than I anticipated and it started to get dark. What a nightmare.

And I'm not even talking about the back seat, which by this time had become a teenage war zone. Even our cleverly devised rotation system, which gave each of them the opportunity to sit in the middle was not working. We arrived in Lusaka mud-spattered, famished and bone-tired. We couldn't get dinner – everything was closed for the night. The children had to eat bully beef out of a tin. I drank Mosi beer. It wasn't much of an improvement on St Louis, but at least it was alcoholic.

I tossed restlessly the entire night – sleepless in Lusaka – afraid that the customs official might be powerful enough to prevent us from leaving Zambia the next day. Breakfast was a quick take away at a petrol station on the outskirts of the city. To fill up cost more than R600, while only the previous day I had paid R180 for a tank of petrol in Botswana. The 550 kilometres to the border took us longer than seven hours as the roads were badly potholed. The only distraction was the regular roadblocks where I had to make a contribution to a variety of officials. The guy with the dark glasses and the fetish-like pieces of dried animal skin, bones (hopefully animal) and other unidentifiable objects on his uniform got more money than any of the others.

Public toilets and hotels like the Road Lodge aimed at the middle-class traveller simply do not exist in most parts of Africa. If you travel with young children a backpacker's lodge is not the kind of place you want to expose them to and most people can't afford $200 to $300 a night for a hotel room. And as I mentioned, the word "camp" does not appear in my dictionary. I once got hold of a permanent marker and had great fun deleting it. I don't even camp at Oppikoppi even though I'm a huge music fan.

That's why we ended up at a Roman-Catholic mission station in Lilongwe where it cost us exactly R50 to accommodate a family of five for the night. For the first time I realised how handy it is to have missionaries around. They go for a no-frills minimalist décor style just like Jesus would have wanted it, but there was warm water and a kitchen where we could cook for the children.

After we paid our entry fee to Club Malawi ($20 for third party cover, R190 for insurance and R10 for something that I can't recall) our cash was disappearing far quicker than I planned. I wasn't so sure whether we could still buy ourselves out of a murder charge. Our food budget was shrinking quickly – you try and feed three young teenage boys when they have nothing else to do but eat. As eating out wasn't an option self-catering was the name of the game.

At the start of day four we had travelled more than 2 000 kilometres and the journey was starting to take its toll. The constant bickering of the boys put stress on my and Pauli's relationship. No matter how hard you try to remain neutral, one's blood is one's blood when it comes to arguments between the children. You always want to protect your own. We had to get to Nkhata Bay soon. We were all suffering from a different kind of cabin fever – we needed a break from being cooped up in the car for hours on end.

Nkhata Bay has a population of just under 10 000 souls. It's a sleepy fishing village where nothing ever happens ... or at least until December when every European backpacker and American aid worker who's worked somewhere in the vicinity descends on the place for the holidays. Everything in Nkhata Bay has two prices: the real one for the locals and the inflated, mzungu price. Naturally I had to pay mzungu prices and I was not happy with this at all. I was also from Africa after all and therefore I should pay the normal price. After a long meeting with the man in charge of the fish market we agreed on a price for the fish that would become our staple food. The fishermen would also bring their catch of the day to us first before taking it to the market. We were their best clients and it was only fair that we should be treated like Most Valued Guests.

The accommodation was slightly more primitive than I had expected. It wasn't huts in the true sense of the word, but rather wooden frames covered by mats. There was no running water and our bath-tub was Lake Malawi where we soaped and washed ourselves. Fortunately, we stayed right on the beach even if it meant taking about 400 stairs to get to the sand. The long drop was at the top of the stairs and the porcelain seat, which was specially brought for us, was stolen within two days. Our car couldn't be parked near our huts and over the next few days it served as an empty canvass for a variety of local taggers.

You're probably thinking it already, so I'll just go ahead and say it: there was very little difference between camping and what we were doing. The only difference was that we did not stay in tents, which ironically would have been more waterproof than our huts.

But the time spent at Lake Malawi did the children a world of good. At night they could walk in the town's streets, play pool in the local bar without being hassled and they could even use their daily allowance to buy things at the market. The boys spent most of the day in their swimming trunks; they went snorkeling and helped the fishermen to weave nets.

Only when one of them told me someone tried to sell them dagga, did I realise there were some unsavoury characters around. They pointed out the man to me and I gave him a good telling-off. I was very upset that he had tried to sell dagga to my 12-year-old son although I have to admit that I did get some for myself. Thing is, if you want to survive a trip with three difficult teenagers who always want to have the last say, it's a good idea to be a little stoned. Your stress levels are much lower, your sense of humour improves and suddenly you are on the same intellectual level as they are.

So life in Nkhata Bay was good. We had fresh food, sunshine, midday naps in a hammock and children who more or less did their own thing (apart from meal times, of course). This was until we were robbed.

From time to time a large steam boat came to Nkhata Bay to off-load people and goods. The morning that the steamer docked, I spotted a few suspect youngsters. But sometimes you are so blinded by your idyllic holiday destination that your Johannesburg radar does not function as it should. And in any case, as we couldn't lock our huts, we were at the mercy of the local people but so far the Nkhata Bay inhabitants treated us like royalty.

The theft happened while we were at a Christmas celebration. There were people who sang and danced, but their performances were neither authentic nor particularly entertaining. The older men looked like English imports. They wore black suits, white shirts and ties with tie pins and all of them wore neat hats. It was so warm that I seriously considered taking off my shirt.

To this day I believe the fact that we decided to return to our huts earlier saved us from far bigger problems. Someone simply walked into the children's hut, which was about thirty metres from ours, and took all their bags. The boys were more upset about their Pokemon and Magic the Gathering cards that they bought over months with their pocket-money than about their stolen clothes. My and Pauli's hut, which would have been next, was untouched.

We were now stuck with three teenagers with only the clothes on their back and a serious cash flow problem. It left a bitter taste in my mouth. I was dirty, seriously pissed off and had had enough of our great African adventure. Our vacation only lasted four days and for the first time the five of us agreed on one thing – the next morning we packed up and left. Only problem was that we were literally thousands of kilometres from home.

A Malawian gangster offered me five airline tickets in exchange for my Merc. He had a cunning plan all right and explained it to me. I could report the car as stolen in South Africa to claim the insurance. It sounded like fraud to me and I declined his offer. We decided to do the 700 kilometres from Nkhata Bay to Blantyre in one go. The boys agreed to the long day in return for an overnight stay in a re-spectable place. We were all in need of room service, television and a decent cup of coffee.

The hamburgers at the Le Merdien Mount Soche in Blantyre were worse than two-day-old McDonalds. If the first hamburger you eat after days without any junk food was this bad, you can imagine what it tasted like. The hotel rooms were $250 each and even though

I had made a promise to the kids, there was no way I could keep it. We had to drag them out of there kicking and screaming while we feverishly devised Plan B. By this time, I felt that the universe owed us a favour. I know we went looking for the ultimate African adventure, but surely everyone deserves a break and a chance to correct their mistakes?

Plan B came in the form of Hostellerie de France, a guesthouse high against a hill with a view of a large part of the city. Apparently it was a firm favourite among Malawian ministers and their mistresses. The owners were two Frenchmen who fled Sierra Leone after one of the wars. One of them looked like a cartoon character of a Frenchman, complete with a rolled moustache and striped shirt.

They must have had a well-developed sixth sense. When they saw us stumbling out of the car, the younger of the two Frenchmen immediately separated the parents from the children. Our room looked like the set of a porno film from the seventies with mirrors everywhere; we had our own veranda and a shower large enough for an orgy. The boys got a large room to share and the Frenchman immediately loaded the Rambo films. They even succeeded in keeping the children away from us during dinner.

The bill came to $134, everything included. The next morning we felt like the whole world smiled with us and so we hit the road to Mozambique. Before we left on the Five Nations Tour, the plan was to drive back along the Mozambican coast and spend a few days there. We quickly changed our minds and took the short cut through the Tete corridor that would get us to Zimbabwe. The main road through the Tete corridor is not for the faint-hearted, especially at night. The sides of the road were littered with overturned vehicles that were stolen in South Africa and never reached their destination. It's a lawless piece of road where Mozambican government officials make the most of the fact that they are so far from the central government. It's as close as you'll ever get to the Wild West in this part of the continent.

Our Mozambican visas were R60 each and we could get them in Blantyre. When we arrived at the border post an interesting sign informed us that all border fees could be paid in South African rand or American dollars. The two amounts were exactly the same: R60 or $60. However the customs official realised that there was a huge difference between the two and insisted on payment in dollars. When I refused I was taken to a small back room where it was carefully explained to me that I was more than welcome to drive around Mozambique if I didn't pay up. I submissively took out $60 for insurance, $30 for third party cover and then an additional $40 to have our passports stamped.

Entrance fee for Club Mozambique: R300 for our visas and $130 at the border. All that for slightly more than an hour's drive.

We were relieved to get going just to be stopped by a policeman who insisted on a full roadworthy test for the car and trailer. The trailer was the worse for wear. Only the very sturdy survive Africa's roads. The electric wiring had stopped working somewhere between Nkhata Bay and Blantyre. I knew that we were in for a spot of trouble if the car and trailer were tested. In a bartering transaction I managed to get back my precious passport, which the policeman held for ransom throughout our negotiation, for $100. At last we were on our way.

We raced through the Tete corridor at 160km/h although we were warned that the speed limit was 100km/h and there were speed traps with spot fines.

Entry to Club Zimbabwe was a surprisingly small amount, only R241, and we had to queue behind a convoy of buses for hours. It was two days before New Year and the whole of southern Africa was on the road. In Harare I made a deal with the manager of a very empty Holiday Inn that we could stay over for R1 000. That night the children channel surfed and ordered room service. Pauli and I went looking for peace and quiet in a bar. The children had had enough of us and we had had enough of them. We were all fed up with the Five Nations tour.

But more than 1 000 kilometres separated Harare from Johannesburg. We interrupted our return trip to spend a night at Greater Zimbabwe, which was enjoyable, but all of us wanted to go home. On 31 December we went through Musina. From there it was full throttle all the way home. Late New Year's Eve we eventually reached our home, kissed the front door and went to bed.

New Year's morning I woke up in my own room in my own house – safe and comfy. For the rest of the day the children walked around as if shell-shocked. We needed a holiday after this holiday. I now understood why people like simple vacations in cities like Cape Town or Durban. And considering the steep drop in my bank balance it might even have been a cheaper option.

Was it traumatic? Of course. Were we to blame for it? Probably. Thousands of backpackers travel through Africa under more severe circumstances and still tell of their great adventures and the good times they had. In general I tend to see my beer glass as half full rather than as half empty, but I have to confess: the Five Nations Tour was a true test for the more positive side of my personality. But then again, many other family holidays have also been rather traumatic. Instead of trying to blame Africa for it, maybe it all comes back to us as parents.

With 20/20 hindsight, I know we learnt a few valuable lessons. Patience is a virtue is one of them. The other is that a self-driving/ self-catering holiday in southern Africa with three teenagers on the back seat of a car brings far greater challenges than many other more carefree holiday options. I also learnt that primitive living conditions while on holiday don't go down well in my world. A warm shower, a flush toilet and some form of room service are my basic requirements. And if I don't have to start a fire to prepare a meal, it is always a bonus.

In the end the holiday did serve its purpose. Our children saw and experienced Africa like few of their school mates have. They wrote colourful essays about their experiences and proudly showed around their passports with all the stamps. To this day they have those passports and talk nostalgically about their big adventure. They even suggested another excursion into Africa.

But so far it's fallen on deaf ears.

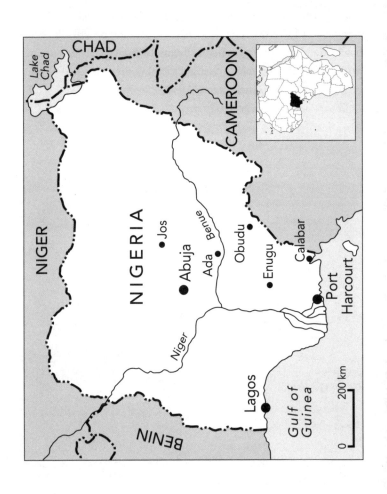

# NIGERIA 101
## Lagos, 2004

**E**VERYTHING YOU'VE EVER heard about Lagos is true. Irrespective of how absurd, ludicrous or miraculous – it's true.

My adventure started after I left the peaceful harmony of OR Tambo and my SAA flight landed on the Murtalla Mohammed Airport squarely in the tropical heat. No one ever took the trouble to change the name of this airport. It was named after a military dictator who came into power with a coup d'etat. Depending on your point of view he was either a war criminal or a visionary reformer who was murdered by a bunch of other generals who didn't like his leadership style.

When we landed, the tough oil worker from Secunda who sat next to me on the flight asked whether it was my first visit to Nigeria. When I said yes and he just smiled wryly the knot at the pit of my stomach tightened. I had heard several stories about how foreigners are treated when entering Nigeria. About the bribery to get through immigration and the import tax of up to 100 dollars on anything you had with you. In addition I only had a tourist visa and I was actually there for work.

I had wanted to do the right thing and get a work visa. But then I heard that the waiting period could be as long as six months due to the intricate paperwork usually associated with an African bureaucracy. I simply didn't have that much time. Two days after I submitted my visa application at the Nigerian consulate in Johannesburg I received my first 419 phishing scam via e-mail.

Two weeks earlier a guy called Albert[6] interrupted my late afternoon drinking binge at the Linden Hotel. I didn't know Albert from a bar of soap and to this day I believe he phoned a wrong number. He kept the call short: "I'm looking for a writer to come and work for me in Nigeria."

I immediately said "yes" without knowing what the job entailed or what I would be paid. And I was clueless of the fears that would haunt me after I did some investigation into other people's work experiences in Nigeria on the internet.

The reason for my over-eagerness was very simple. I was broke and didn't have any jobs lined up in the short term. Besides, the people around me were driving me crazy. A few weeks outside the country would do me a lot of good, I thought. And also, my well-developed sense of adventure kicked in. By saying "yes", I could order another beer as soon as I'd put my phone down.

Johannesburg's afternoon traffic in Fourth Avenue in Linden no longer made me jealous. Moments before the call I'd wished that I was a white collar worker in one of those cars. At least then I'd be certain that there would be money in my bank account at the end of the month. One problem when you work for yourself is that you're always under pressure because you're constantly looking for more work or you have to complete projects that you've already been paid for. Now I could calmly order a Jägermeister with my beer. If only I'd known what it would take to bring back a few American dollar to South Africa …

A few days later I met Albert and his co-producer, Lewis, in the same bar in the Linden Hotel to discuss the job. I still didn't know

---

6  For safety's sake I've given most of the people mentioned in this chapter pseudonyms.

what it was all about, but was looking forward to a uniquely African experience.

Albert was a daredevil kind of guy – an arrogant fellow who could easily have found his niche in the army. Someone who liked to assert his position of power. Lewis was extremely practical and could solve any problem. He came from a railway background – a man who has already owned and lost a Ferrari. Lewis was the Mac-Gyver type you'd like to have around when your ship runs aground on a deserted island.

The combination of the two lifted my spirits. I was asked to be the writer and psychological manipulator[7] for a new reality television programme in Nigeria. It would be the first of its kind in Nigeria. They didn't offer any more details. Come to Lagos and let's see what we have to do was the general (and only) strategy.

So now I was standing in the queue at the airport in Lagos among a group of jittery South Africans who couldn't stand still. Unlike other countries the customs people sit on a stage. When you hand over your passport, the officials look down on you. There was a line on the floor in front of the stage. You were not allowed to cross the line; you had to lean over to hand over your passport. If your foot were to touch the line, you were sent to the back of the queue.

Now it sounds hilarious, then it wasn't.

Fortunately I was accompanied by a former soldier who went by the name of "Captain". He was the kind of guy who saw a job opportunity in the nightmarish confusion of Murtalla Mohammed and firmly entrenched himself amidst the chaos and fears of the foreigners. Captain's rank also became his name and he walked

---

7  If you think everything on reality television happens naturally, you're dead wrong. Keep on reading to the next chapter if you want to find out how unreal it really is.

though the airport building as if it belonged to him – who knows, that might even have been the case. The former soldier now spent his days guaranteeing a safe passage through the airport to those visitors who could afford his services. For the right fee he made sure no one hassled you, that you didn't have to pay any "good days" and that nobody scratched around in your luggage before you officially entered the country.

The reason why he could do this of course was because he paid part of his fee to a senior customs and immigration official. The word therefore came from higher up that Captain's clients were not be touched. But if you didn't have Captain with you, you were fair game and anyone could pressure you for money. By paying Captain you at least knew who had to be paid and this certainly made me feel safer.

The airport was dirty and dilapidated and it was obvious that the Nigerians did not pursue a culture of maintenance. Long, long ago, perhaps around the oil boom of the 1970s, somebody built a grand building, but that was possibly the last time anyone gave any attention to it. There were broken windows and closed doors to offices that hadn't seen the light of day for years. In the few offices that were open, the furniture was shabby and broken. There were no computers. Everything was documented with pen and paper. The whole place smelled of stale food.

Welcome to Lagos, Nigeria.

If you survive the nightmare ordeal and get outside, you'll realise that the air-conditioning was actually switched on. Tropical heat has advantages and disadvantages. Face and body cream are no longer necessary, but deodorant becomes essential. You soon get used to sweat patches and dirty nails – my two pet phobias.

The shock of the heat outside the airport was quickly replaced by the shock of the scene that met me. If you don't have a flight to catch, you're not allowed inside the airport building. The exit was surrounded by guard rails that were manned by police officers in black uniforms, dark sunglasses and the omnipresent show of force, the AK47. A mass of people strained against the guard rails. They ranged from money agents and taxi drivers to drivers with signs to pick up passengers. The noise was unbearable. The police thrashed those hard of hearing with batons, sticks and rubber whips.

The moment you cross over to the other side of the guard rails you become fair game. Everyone pulls, pushes and shoves you to get a bit of business. I felt like a rock star minus the bodyguards. Unlike Rwanda I was here without government protection. I felt exposed and terrified. Unlike Rwanda I had to behave and adhere to the laws of the country.

My white skin made me a larger target in Nigeria and that's why I took out more insurance against kidnapping in Johannesburg. It was a last minute thing, which I didn't regret doing. I was covered up to and including a ransom of one million dollars. A security advisor in Johannesburg told me that most kidnappers know what the maximum insurance is and therefore never ask for more than one million dollars. Actually, the insurance premium was much cheaper than I thought it would be. I could only hope that should I be kidnapped, the company wouldn't start negotiating with the kidnappers to save on the ransom money.

At the airport I met the other two South Africans on the team. They were from Cape Town. That should have made the alarm bells go off. Jenny was the producer of the programme who had to make sure that everything went smoothly and that we were paid – a job at which she would fail miserably over the next few weeks. Our production manager, a position that is usually filled by a local person with contacts, was Jenny's son, Jamie. He was a lad fresh out of rehab with a few issues he hadn't dealt with yet. The Greater Power who created Jamie's personality did it by the book alright – a psychology textbook that detailed each and every characteristic that would irritate the hell out of most people … including Nigerians.

There are between 13 and 17 million residents in Lagos. The figures vary because of corruption during the previous census. Apparently the money for the census disappeared into somebody's pocket so they opted for a rough estimate. One of the city's problems is that it's made up of a lot of islands (hence the name "Lagos", which is Portuguese for "island" – as with many other places in Africa the Portuguese colonised it first). The islands are connected by long bridges. When 13 million people move around on roads that last saw any maintenance in the 1970s, you can expect some fairly serious problems. Due to accommodation shortages people built wooden huts on poles in the water. The huts don't have flush toilets or electricity, but in the morning the residents get up, dress up and row their boats ashore, where they catch a taxi or *okada* and go to work. The minimum wage when I visited was R350 a month.

The roads were hardly sufficient for the number of road users and the drainage system was last cleaned in the 1970s. When it rained, we drove through streets so full of water that a boat would have had a better chance to get around than a car.

The drive from the airport, at ten o'clock at night, lasted four hours. It was a nightmare of hooting vehicles, seven cars next to each other when there was only room for four, and police road blocks with the sole purpose to collect bribes.

Among the mayhem and madness were the *okadas*: small, Chinese 125cc motorcycles that carried three to six people (plus luggage) and recklessly wormed their way through the hypercongestion and exhaust fumes.

The passengers did not wear crash helmets and on most *okadas* the handlebars were not transverse, but bent upwards so that they could negotiate narrower gaps. Traffic in Italy is a breeze compared to what happens on the roads in Nigeria. Here everyone drives like South African taxi drivers, except of course the Nigerian taxi drivers themselves. They are a law unto themselves. Most taxis had taken off their sliding doors so that the passengers could get in and out quicker. Nigeria was clearly not a country of quality, but rather quantity. All the cars were dented.

For those who could afford it there were a variety of helicopter companies that would transport you to wherever you wanted to go.

My first impressions of Lagos:
1. The entire city was in urgent need of a coat of paint.
2. It would be a simple affair to die of carbon monoxide poisoning – you just need to be stuck in traffic long enough.
3. The sidewalks were not maintained and because it's the tropics, they looked like overgrown gardens.
4. Everything was rusted and the whole country was held together with wire.
5. There is a big difference between what is regarded as roadworthy in Lagos and in the rest of the world.
6. If you have a blue light on your car people have to make way for you even if there isn't anywhere to go. If they don't give way, the police beat dents in the sides of the cars to make them hurry up.

But I have to admit that I didn't get my first impressions of Lagos on my way from the airport to the hotel. I arrived after sunset and in Lagos you can't see anything at night, because there's no electricity. The last person who leaves Nigeria need not switch off the lights, because they were never on.

Strange but true, power is a scarce commodity in a city with 13 million people in one of the largest oil producing countries in Africa. Everything that's electric and working is powered by private generators. Middle-class houses that cost close to R1 million have their own generators. Most houses have two generators, which work in shifts of four hours. This means that someone has to switch them on or off after their shift. When our very difficult shoot on Snake Island was wrapped up my Nigerian colleague didn't even want to go home, because it meant that he had to get up at ungodly hours to change generators to prevent them from burning out.

According to the contract, the work for the television programme would last three weeks. On the first morning at the international advertising agency contracted to handle the production, we soon realised that their idea of a reality programme differed a great deal from what we believed it should be. In addition, there was no structure or plan – only the hope that if they stuck a whole lot of people who didn't know each other in an office they would quickly slap something together. We had to start shooting the programme the following week, but they didn't even have a location.

For those of you who are not in the know a little background: when you make a television programme you usually get money from a television station. The work is given to a production house who then accepts the responsibility to do everything and deliver the programme on time. The *Gulder Ultimate Search* (the name of the programme) would work differently.

Gulder is the most popular beer in West Africa. The brewery would finance the production. The advertising agency would be in control of the production to make sure their trade name was protected and the right image conveyed. The agency would then appoint a production house to do the actual work. When the programme was finished, the client would broadcast it on various television stations.

Gulder belonged to the largest brewery in Nigeria, Nigerian Breweries, which forms part of Heineken in the Netherlands. It therefore took quite some time to get the right people to make the decisions.

The idea was that the programme, rather than ordinary adverts, would be used to give the product a kick start in a declining beer market. The advertising agency was used to making adverts, a process that is very different and takes more time than it does to make a television programme. With an advert each shot is worked out and thought out precisely (or that's what they lead you to believe). Reality television is about content, not necessarily about how pretty things look – although you can achieve that as well if you plan properly.

Good planning doesn't often happen in Nigeria. This project was no exception. Pretty soon it was clear that it would take at least three weeks just to get the plan going. The camera men had no idea how to shoot a reality programme, the sound men didn't know how to record it and the advertising company didn't know how to make it.

It seemed that we were in for an uphill battle. Lagos, already a difficult city to work in, didn't seem to be on our side. Just moving from meeting to meeting sometimes took us three hours in the congested traffic. And that was only in one direction. An entire day could be taken up by a single meeting. On the very first day we arrived back at the flat way past midnight.

My flat mate, and one of the great creative minds at the agency, was a South African called Maritz. His creative brain was also an addicted brain. When he still was a big shot in the South African advertising industry his consumption was legendary. But he got his life on track, and he quit booze and drugs. But he developed a new addiction: women. Every night there was a different one who stayed over for R100. Short, tall, thin, stupid or clever, Maritz wasn't picky and never heard of quality control when it came to women. By the end of the first television series he was abruptly fired in a uniquely non-confrontational way: a letter was pushed underneath the flat door. He didn't even go back to the office; he went straight back to South Africa.

In Nigeria there isn't any legislation that protects workers. If your boss arrives at work one morning all grumpy or in a foul mood and you irritate him, you could very well be fired on the spot. This situation means that people are inordinately submissive. Everyone is too scared to venture an opinion, in case it's the wrong one. If the boss laughs at a joke everybody laughs along. This wasn't exactly conducive to creativity and it wasn't an environment in which I felt comfortable. I decided to do things the standard Deon way and see what would happen. My feeling was that the worst thing that could happen was that they could send me home.

Then they asked for my passport.[8]

Now we all know that the rule is never to give your passport to someone in a foreign country, except when you enter and leave the country. Your passport is your key to freedom of movement. At that time the novelty of being in another country was wearing off and a cold hand clamped around my heart.

Foreign country where corruption ranks among the top ten in the world – check. No passport – check. No money – check.

Money soon became a problem. In Nigeria everything is based on cash transactions. No one trusted the banks, because they usually went bankrupt when the bank owners had stolen enough money. They,

---

8  I had to hand my passport to the advertising company as my visa wasn't valid for a long enough period. They would apply for an extension via official channels. My passport was only returned to me on the day I left Nigeria. Everything went smoothly when I departed, because Captain escorted me out. On my next visit I was almost arrested and had to pay a fat "fine", because some overzealous official noticed that the visa extension from my previous visit was falsified.

of course, were protected by their friends in government who also helped themselves to a large chunk of the bank's change. So you knew you would be paid soon when someone pitched with a large, thick, brown envelope. That was if you were paid in naira. When you were paid in dollars the envelope was usually much thinner.

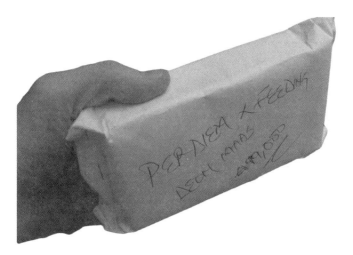

Two people were involved in the payout process. They folded out a small table, opened the envelope and counted your 100 dollar notes one by one. Before they gave them to you, the junior of the two took out a specially designed koki pen and drew a line on each note. If the pen left a line on the note, the note was forged. If there wasn't a line, it was the real product straight from Uncle Sam. It was a painstaking process but fortunately I never had to wait very long because I was paid so little.

When I heard we were going to be paid directly by the Nigerians instead of the agency in Cape Town who hired us, I realised that the payouts were not going to go smoothly. Our first per diem (daily allowance) was hundreds of rand short. When I enquired about the shortfall, Innocent, the Nigerian agency's paymaster, reckoned the money could have fallen out in his car. The envelope was stapled but after a short search he indeed found the missing money on the floor of his car from where it had been miraculously teleported from the stapled envelope.

The weekly dollar wage payments didn't go much better. Usually the money was paid too late or it was short and you didn't have a leg to stand on when you tried to complain. You couldn't go to the police or an attorney. You were working in Nigeria illegally and no one was interested in helping you. It was only after I suddenly developed acute writers' arthritis that the problem was quickly solved. I'd already had the first tentative attacks in Lagos, but it became a full-blown problem on the island where we shot the series.

Writers' arthritis is a terrible affliction. Your hands turn around so that your fingers touch your wrists. It's almost impossible to type or even write. The only cure is to receive payment. The sulks don't do any good and even if the writer and the lady making the tea (in Nigeria it is a man) are on the same level, people quickly find out that they can't do without a writer. Everyone thinks they can write, until push comes to shove. Soon my payments were up to date and the amounts correct. I could concentrate on my work again.

A guide to Nigerian English:

| Nigerian word | Acceptable English word |
|---|---|
| Biro | Pen |
| Waterstopper | Bath plug |
| Yesterday night | Last night |
| Tomorrow's tomorrow | The day after tomorrow |
| Tax | Task |
| Foil | Fuel |
| Flash | Missed call |

| | |
|---|---|
| Onion | Nipple |
| Well done | Good morning |
| You're welcome | Good morning |
| Ease myself | *Draw your own conclusions …* |

It was very amusing, until you wanted to get something done without knowing what these quaint phrases meant. And by the way, if you want to use a "water stopper" in Nigeria, take one with you. They don't sell them there. As a travel tip in case you do forget to take one, I suggest large quantities of toilet paper. Just don't ask for toilet paper in the shop. They'll look at you quizzically. But they'll know what you want if you ask for "tissue".

South Africans are extremely finicky and nowhere will you hear them moan louder than in bars all over Africa. They are vocal about how many ice cubes they want, where the ice was made and the type of whisky they want to drink.

In Nigeria consumers' choices, to put it mildly, are very limited. In Lagos there are a few expat shops that offer a smallish choice of delicacies from the rest of the world. Here you can choose between Belgian chocolate, Swiss cheese, and for some reason, English biscuits. Forget about the rest. The question isn't what kind of whisky you want, but whether there is any whisky available. This even applied to some of the better hotels. Cocktails, Jägermeister and tequila were words they did not know.

In the hotels something peculiar happens: Nigerian women appear out of the blue the moment you walk into the bar. In general decent women don't hang out in the bars, only those looking for a few naira or even a marriage – even to someone they don't particularly like, as long as it gets them out of their personal difficulties. You can understand their predicament, considering that about 90% of the people don't have jobs and even graduates keep on studying because their dads don't know anyone who can organise them a job.

What made these women truly impressive was that they simply didn't take "no" for an answer. They didn't leave you alone. You say you're married. Doesn't work. You say you're gay. Doesn't work either (it's illegal in Nigeria; so be careful if you want to use that excuse). One night after trying to get rid of a very smart, cute and sexy young lady for about 30 minutes, I told her that I wasn't interested in her because she was fat and ugly. She still wouldn't leave.

These women were surrounded by an aura of desperation. They would literally do anything for a better future.

One night I sat in the bar with the director, Lewis. Having a drink with Lewis was very boring, because he didn't really drink. His idea of a big night out was two tots of brandy neatly spaced out an hour or three from each other. The advantage was that he always had a few extra naira of his per diem if I didn't have anything left, and he was willing to pay for a drink or two. I enjoyed his company, but there's something very sad about gradually drinking yourself into a stupor because you're far from home while your drinking buddy is stone cold sober.

Anyway, we were sitting in the bar. There were high wooden panels between the tables. I was vaguely aware that two women were sitting behind us at their own table. One of them got up to go to the toilet. When she came back, she left a piece of paper on our table and went back to her friend. Lewis and I looked at each other nonplussed. I opened the note and read: "My name is Blessing, CALL ME, 08030732320. I will like to meet you guys again. Thank's (sic)."

I never did contact Blessing, but always wondered what would have happened if I did. Would she really have done anything I expected of her in exchange for money? Or could she have been curious to meet an *oyibo* (white man in Yoruba) — there aren't many of them around — or was she really so desperate that she would invite a total stranger to phone her? Neither Lewis nor I are oil-paintings (sorry, Lewis). It wasn't as if we got her hormones racing with our devastatingly good looks. We didn't even exchange a single word. So she couldn't have fallen for our charming banter.

My flat mate, Maritz, didn't have the same moral qualms that I did in matters of the flesh. I was dragged to bars like the Ynot and Thistle where the only Nigerian men were the blokes who applied the rules of the club. They were huge, dressed in black suits and made it perfectly clear who was ruling the roost. You might have the money to take the girls home, but they made the rules.

The interesting thing is that these girls weren't real prostitutes. They didn't look or dress like prostitutes. They were well-read and one even knew a few Afrikaans words — which made me think that the Voortrekkers trekked much farther than I imagined, even if it was a century or two later. The girls were mainly university students who hung out in the bars in the hope of paying next month's class fees.

The one thing they did have in common with prostitutes was their determined search for money. One of them sat her cute bum down on the chair next to me and put her hand on my knee. I removed it and made it clear that I wasn't interested. I think she was surprised, because the only reason why white men went to this particular bar was for the promise she just made to me. She repeated the gesture and each time I removed her hand. After half an hour she saw it wasn't going to work, excused herself from the table and asked for 2 000 naira (about R100). I was surprised and wanted to know why. She said she needed money for a taxi home, but I stuck to my guns and said I told her right from the start I wasn't interested.

A few seconds later one of the steroid freaks in a black suit appeared to solve the problem. At first he was very intimidating. I told him I wasn't a European woosie; that I was from Johannesburg. He asked whether I knew his brother who lived there. Unfortunately I didn't, but he removed the girl. The rest of the night I sat alone at a table in a crowded club and studied the foreplay rituals of fat and lonely white men. I don't remember much, because the whisky was cheap. But I do remember that I had a good time.

> "At least five people died while several others were seriously injured when two Fedeco commercial buses had a head-on collision in the middle of the mainland bridge on Monday. The accident occurred at about noon when the two buses, one of which was driving against the traffic to beat a traffic jam, collided head on and somersaulted several times."
>
> *Vanguard*, April 2004
>
> The bridge is a highway with a ridge. On the highway the driver of the one bus drove on the wrong side against oncoming traffic to get past a traffic jam. I saw it with my own two eyes.

Apart from the odd evening out, the good times in Lagos were few and far between. The chief officer of Nigerian Breweries was an old school African dictator who managed his company in the same way

Idi Amin, Teodoro Obiang (president of Equatorial Guinea since 1979), and that Chavez guy of Venezuela ruled their various countries.

One of our contacts at the advertising agency was a fellow called Bobby. One of his jobs was to make sure we were paid. Bobby looked like one of those bullfrogs at the reptile exhibition at Hartebeespoort Dam. The only time they moved was when they ate. They didn't have a backbone, their mouths were flabby and the lower lip protruded past the upper lip.

Bobby and I will never be friends. I don't think Bobby will ever be friends with anyone. There might be a very good reason why Bobby's wife stayed in Australia and he lives in Lagos. In general I'm not fond of advertising agency people. They'll suck on anything to make an extra rand or two. Bobby was no exception, but he took my antipathy towards this kind of person to a much higher level. Bobby treated people like used toilet paper – excluding, of course, those who were more important than him. One day while we were stuck in traffic, he rolled down the window and spat on a beggar. "The world is divided between cowboys and Indians," he explained to me, "and we don't care about the Indians."

Dale Carnegie of *How to Win Friends and Influence People* fame did not feature in his vocabulary. At the same time Bobby, like most Nigerians, was a faithful church-goer who regularly used the term *ambe olorun*. *Ambe olorun* means to plead with God. When he started using this term it had the same effect as another Nigerian favourite, "I beg", which is often used as an interjection to tell you to forget about trying to change their minds and accept the inevitable. When Bobby started pleading you knew you were going to lose the argument. Let's just say he had a black belt in pleading.

What I therefore had to contend with was the following: the unpleasant people from the agency, a programme that hadn't taken on any shape, a client who apparently wanted to shoot down his own project and a sex slave as a flat mate who dragged me to places where people sell their souls for tuition fees. All of a sudden the reality of my adventure wasn't as pleasant as the theory over a Jagie and a beer at the Linden Hotel.

At the same time I had actually started to like Lagos. It wasn't as dangerous as everyone would lead you to believe, but it was definitely crazier than anything I'd ever experienced before. According to one theory Lagos wasn't dangerous at all and the stories told about its dangers were in fact rumours started by the residents themselves. The idea was to limit the number of areas that visitors would feel comfortable to visit on their own and to ensure that they paid locals to take them around. It created jobs and enabled more people to squeeze you for money. It stimulated the economy. In Lagos no one would hurt you if they could make money out of you. Why ruin a future job opportunity by hurting someone if you could get something from them?

The city has a rhythm and beat all of its own. My relationship with this dirty, noisy place is difficult to put into words. Pauli says that the smell of something or someone will make you decide whether you like them or not. You decide whether to sleep with someone if you like their smell. If that was the case, I would never have fallen in love with Lagos.

More Lagos moments that I experienced first-hand:

1.  A policeman fired his AK47 at a busload of people because the driver ignored his instructions.

2.  Two guys jumped out of a church bus in congested traffic on the highway and broke the windscreen wipers of the bakkie next to them because they objected to the owner's driving.

3. Two policemen dragged a truck driver who caused a traffic jam out of his vehicle by his feet, thrashed him with batons and then casually strolled away to try and sort out the traffic problem.

4. Polio sufferers from the Muslim north of the country propel themselves on home-made skateboards through the busy traffic to beg. They only have a torso and arms. When they knock at your car window, you have to look down to see them. The imams didn't allow polio sufferers to get vaccinations as this is ostensibly against the principles of the Koran.

5. I saw a burn victim whose upper arm was burnt into his torso.

Lagos kind of reminds me of a girl you know, who is fat and ugly, but you still want to go to bed with. Maybe because she's interesting. You know your friends are going to ridicule you, but you couldn't care. That's how I felt about Lagos. I tried to justify my love for the city – especially after I'd had a few beers and was eventually starting to tell the truth – but then I accepted that no one else shared my passion, including those who lived there.

By the way, in Nigeria beer is only sold in one size: 600 ml. You'll pay R20 for a tot of whisky, but you'll pay the same price for the whole bottle in a bottle store. Another nifty travellers tip for when you find yourself there one day. The chance that you'll end up there because someone offers you a job for more money than you'll ever earn in South Africa is increasing daily.

… But back to my story.

Any South African who complains about the state of our country should be sentenced to two months labour in Lagos. When they return they'll never complain again. Unlike South Africans who moan about everything, Lagos' residents, against all expectations, simply accept the situation for what it is and make a plan. They drive around the potholes in the streets, they have a plan B for power outages and to top it off they generally make a success of their lives. If you leave work at a time when traffic is so badly congested that it's impossible to make it back to the office in time the next day, you simply sleep in your car. In which other city would people be willing to do that?

What fanned my love for Lagos was the nightlife. Not my flat mate's idea of nightlife, the real thing. It was in Lagos that I met Chidi Mokeme, Nollywood star supreme and the only man I know with a belt buckle with his name in diamanté.

Chidi was the presenter of the *Gulder Ultimate Search* and my saving grace in Lagos. We immediately clicked like long-lost brothers. He dragged me out of the pit of depressing expat bars and introduced me to the top end of the nightlife in Lagos. Chidi was the kind of guy who could charm both sexes but, unlike many other well-known people, he only used his charm to do good. For instance, he was sincerely interested in the policeman's story at one of the road blocks and listened to it attentively. Yes, it also meant that he wouldn't have to pay a bribe but he really seemed to care.

Chidi's Mercedes S500 regularly made late-night appearances in Lagos' streets and club-goers knew him well. He had three cell phones and he constantly received text messages. Many of the calls were from people he didn't know, ordinary fans who got his number somewhere. Everyone was treated with respect and he never took advantage of a situation by taking them to bed.

One Sunday night after midnight he called me to say that we were going clubbing. I knew Lagos was a late-night city that never slept, but to go out on a Sunday night after midnight was a first for me. In Lagos it was nothing out of the ordinary.

Club Extreme had a stylish sign on the gate of its VIP parking area. The sign requested people with cars worth less than 100 000 dollars not to park there. Like most clubs in Lagos, this club was owned and controlled by Lebanese. Lebanese are just about the only *oyibos* who have Nigerian citizenship. They control large sections of the economy, thanks of course to the necessary "happy weekend" payments to those in high places.

It cost 100 dollars to get into the club. We didn't pay. Chidi had his own corner on the side of the bar, which was fenced off with a red velvet rope. Only he was allowed to drink there. If he wasn't there, it was kept empty. Chidi positioned himself between me and the rest of the bar and I soon saw why. Within minutes there was a bunch of girls who wanted to chat to him. Chidi made a joke or two with them, but it was soon clear that most of them weren't interested in conversation. Then Chidi lost interest and sent them on their way with a sharp remark and a smile. Most of the girls were beautiful, but at one stage two appeared who were simply stunning. Model babes. A month or two ago one of them was on the cover of the *Elle* magazine. These two thought they would succeed where the others failed. To try and convince Chidi one lay down on the bar counter, drew her friend closer and started to play kinky licking games.

Chidi decided it was time to move on to the VIP section. Entry to the VIP section cost 1 000 dollars. We didn't pay. A bottle of ice-cold Absolut was served. Chidi pointed out all the big boys of Lagos. This one owned a bank, that one was a big shot in government. Everyone was surrounded by at least two or three beautiful young girls who were clearly not their wives. So much for escaping the expat bar scene. These people seemed slightly happier though. I had to make peace with the fact that this was the way things worked in Lagos.

Our trip back to the hotel coincided with Lagos' notorious morning traffic. Chidi and I finished the bottle of Absolut among the morning hooting accompanied by the sounds of Limp Bizkit, Ice-T, Linkin Park and a variety of other kick-ass music from the club that was still resounding in our ears. Few people knew Lagos as a party city. It could be that the first layers of the party spirit came off easily. Here people more often partied to forget than to celebrate life.

Nigeria is a country with a truckload of problems. The first is its oil resources. In the 1970s when the first oil fields were discovered and Lagos experienced the economic boom that goes with oil discoveries, EMI still had a studio there where Paul McCartney and his band Wings recorded their album *Band on the Run*. Everyone was looking forward to a bright future and everyone reckoned they would share in the riches. People stopped working and no longer cultivated their fields in anticipation of the wealth that would come. It didn't happen. The money and power were quickly concentrated in the hands of a small number of people. The super rich made sure that nobody else came close to it.

The more I talked to Nigerians the more I heard the sigh that the British should have stayed longer. The general feeling was that had the Brits still been there when oil was discovered, the income from oil sales would have been utilised better and spread more equally. As is the case in most Third World countries where oil is discovered, it caused more problems than progress for the average Nigerian.

It created the ideal climate for corruption, which may have started at the top, but nonetheless filtered its way down to the lowest level. If you wanted to share in the wealth, you had to give up a portion of your income to grease palms. If you wanted to take a photograph of someone you had to pay them. If you wanted to make an appointment with someone you had to pay his secretary for the privilege of seeing him.

One of the reasons why Nigerian newspapers publish so few stories about crime is that journalists are paid to do a story about something, and not necessarily by the newspaper. If I didn't like someone, I could give you a fat envelope with the story I'd written and it was a done deal. One of my Nigerian friends couldn't understand my surprise that he'd slipped the immigration official 50 dollars in his passport. "But he's allowing me to come back into my country," was the argument. The fact that it was the immigration official's job and that he had to do it, my Nigerian friend couldn't understand.

> "The Minister of the Federal Capital Territory, Mallam Nasir el-Rufai, made it known on Tuesday in Abuja that 42 000 ghostworkers had been uncovered in the civil service."
>
> *This Day*, May 2004

Today Nigeria imports food but it's got some of the most fertile soil I have ever seen – it's in the tropics, it's warm, it gets lots and lots of rain. It's the kind of soil most farmers dream about. The oil-rich Nigeria also has a constant shortage of petrol. Days and weeks sometimes passed and the economy almost ground to a halt due to fuel shortages. The corruption was so bad that a big shot in the navy sold one of their war ships for millions and pocketed the money. Everybody knew who he was, but no one ever did anything about it.

But what can you expect of a country that has had a series of military presidents, of whom some are still very powerful? In the seventies general Olusegun Obasanjo came into power after the military ruler Murtalla Mohammed died in a failed coup. In 1979 he handed the power to a civil government, but in the early eighties the army again took control. In the late nineties Obasanjo was democratically elected as president after the military dictator Sani Abacha died of a heart attack. Abacha's death was allegedly caused by an overdose of Viagra when he had sex with two Indian prostitutes. After his death government realised that he and his family had embezzled about three billion dollars. The Abacha family was eventually persuaded to return one billion dollars to the government.

What a country!

And of course everyone was in church on Sunday. In Nigeria churches are more than just a place where you go to worship. This is where you show off your new clothes and your new Hummer. Pastors appear on magazine covers and are treated like pop stars. They all preached one message: the more you love God, the more money you will have. And don't forget that the 10% you give to the church will help you get to heaven.

Apart from problems with oil and corruption, the second major problem is religious differences. The relationship between the Christians in the south and the Muslims in the north has always been precarious. To spice up the mix even further there are the animists, but they are mostly left in peace, because most Nigerians are scared of them. They believe the animists can cast a spell on you.

In Nigeria you often see men holding their penises. This custom started in the 1970s when an epidemic of "penis theft" hit the country between 1975 and 1977.

Men suddenly started "losing" their penises. The precise meaning of "lose" is somewhat difficult to explain. The penises weren't cut off. They simply disappeared. Dr Sunday Ilechukwu wrote in the *Transcultural Psychiatric Review* that although he could see the "victim's" penis, the victim and the man who stole it, could not. Juju, a local form of witchcraft, was to blame for this. In some cases the penises disappeared and only reappeared after the "spell" was lifted.

In the early 1990s mass hysteria reared its ugly head (pardon the pun) yet again. In April 2001 twelve people were murdered by vigilantes after they had been accused of penis theft. *The Nation*, a prominent newspaper, published the following report on 30 June 2009 under the heading "Fear grips Taraba over loss of genitals":

"Over 22 cases of missing genitals have been reported to the state's police command, a development that has forced some residents to flee the area. Police spokesman Sani Baba told reporters that 10 suspects have been arrested but added that 'no scientific proof has been established'. Four people have been reportedly killed over the 'missing parts flu'."

Muslims and Christians regularly fight amongst each other. Antipathy is stirred up by the pastors and imams when they feel their numbers are under threat. Then, like in Rwanda, it's neighbour against neighbour. After a few weeks everything returns to normal, until the next riot erupts.

In the Boko Haram riots of 2009 in the north of the country Yusuf Mohammed (his parents are to blame for his unoriginal name), a Muslim leader who championed a Taliban-like state, was summarily executed. Over a period of three days another 780 of his followers were mowed down by the police, who, by the way, do not place much stock in tear gas and rubber bullets, but have access to loads of AK47 ammunition. Most of the followers were unarmed. In a news report the chief of police said the following about the executions: "Anyone who kills must definitely die, no matter how. We should not have pity for them at all. They have killed and should be killed too."

One policeman was killed in the riots. The weapons that the police allegedly retrieved from the mosque before they blew it up, was as real as George W Bush's weapons of mass destruction. The whole country knew that the riots were going to happen. There were even newspaper reports about it, but the army and police chose to ignore it; they were too busy collecting bribes from motorists. Why do our jobs if we can get money elsewhere?

The third large problem in Nigeria is the friction between the three largest ethnic groups, the Yoruba, Hausa and Igbo, but it's a terribly long story, which I'll tell some other day.

Quick facts about Lagos and Nigeria:

1. The delicate art of graffiti is not practiced in Lagos. You won't see graffiti anywhere. All taxis in the state of Lagos have to be painted yellow. Each state's taxis have a different colour.

2. There are statues of historical figures everywhere that haven't been cleaned in years, but vandals don't touch them.

3. There aren't any movie theatres in Lagos. All Nollywood movies are immediately available on DVD. The master copy is sold to pirates because they have the best distribution network.

4. The beaches are littered with plastic and rubbish from ships waiting to enter the harbour.

5. One of Lagos' beaches is divided into two. One side is used for church services where they baptise people, and the other side is an open air bordello with lots of bars.

6. After Hollywood and Bollywood, Nollywood produces the most movies worldwide.

7. The average Nollywood movie is shot in four days.

8. At the Thistle bar there is a cover band that plays "Ipi Tombi" and "Living Next Door to Alice" as a medley.

9. Nigeria has more than sixty newspapers, more than any other country in Africa.

10. There are 250 different ethnic groups in Nigeria.

Despite the niggling of the client and the agency, our programme had begun to take shape. The hype around the programme reached fever pitch thanks to the excellent media coverage. Because it was Nigeria's first reality television programme and peculiar to the country, a sense of self-worth started to develop and the belief that Nigerians can indeed do something for themselves. At that point the agency decided to remove the South African profiles from the website. We became anonymous.

My ego was at an all-time low, and I couldn't be bothered. I was there to make a programme, be paid and then go home. I lost all hope that we would create anything worthwhile that I could put on my show reel. I was a pen for hire – a professional writer fully armed with a computer and a hectic imagination who hoped that his story line would go down big.

By this time the website was getting 100 000 hits per hour from people who wanted to take part in the programme. Money and fame offered two ways of rising above the masses. It seemed that our programme would be a hit; all we had to do now was actually make it. After three weeks, the period they initially thought it would take to conceptualise a programme, get participants and do a shoot of twenty-one days, we had a basic concept and were ready to begin screening the hundreds of applications.

The idea for the programme was straightforward. It was like mix-ing a cocktail really: a dash of *Survivor*, a splash of *Fear Factor* and half a bottle of Nigeria – all shaken up. Not one of the limitations that other countries place on the content of TV programmes applied to Nigeria. You can slaughter chickens and goats on television to your heart's content and place people in chains (if you do this to black people in any other country it would be seen as symbolic of the slave trade; even the American *Survivor* wouldn't allow it). In addition, being used to rough treatment, no one would bemoan their plight. The general feeling was that you had to suffer to become rich and famous. And Nigerians did know how to suffer.

Something that would otherwise be a *wahala* (problem) was *no wahala*.

As the writer I was given a list of authentic Nigerian expressions. They reckoned that if I put some of these phrases in my script, the viewers would believe that the writer was Nigerian. They failed to realise that Nigerian English is so full of false metaphors, even in the most serious newspapers, that most of the time it's impossible to understand what anyone's saying.

A few highlights from the list:
- To be a man is not a day job (life is tough)
- No paddy for jungle (life doesn't do you any favours)
- Lepa shandy (a thin girl)
- Chop up (rich person)
- God dey (hope)
- No shakings (everything is alright)
- Shine your eye (be sharp)
- No kain (no problem)
- E-easy (things are tough)
- Smooth operator (cunning guy)
- Sharp guy (clever guy)

The fact that the last two expressions were on the list is proof that Nigerians in general believe the rest of the world is dumb and that no one will ever understand them.·

Hundreds of people flocked to the auditions. It was not an orderly process. No one knew what we were looking for or how the whole thing would work out. I desperately wanted to get out of Lagos. By then I had been relieved of my money by too many scoundrel waiters and the only barber in the country who could cut "white hair". My joke that I didn't really have "white hair" but "red hair" went right over the Lebanese's head.

The plan was to take ten victims – sorry, participants – to an island and leave them in the jungle. Snake Island was about thirty minutes by boat from Lagos. Every so often, to make for entertaining television, one participant would get chucked off the island.

At this stage the ten participants (six men and four women) who were still on the mainland, were already behaving like super stars, complete with sunglasses at night because of the media hype. They stayed at a five star hotel and for a few days before their departure they could do whatever they pleased. This is a technique that producers of reality television often use. It's a simple trick that works every time: make the participants feel important for a while and then suddenly drop them in the middle of nowhere. The shock is so much greater.

Director Albert's plan to get the participants to the island had interesting results. We had to get them onto a boat, with their sunglasses, give them each a cocktail and pretend they were going on another fun cruise. In the middle of nowhere we would switch off the boat's engine, load them in two canoes and make them find Snake Island with the aid of a compass. On paper it looked like a grand idea, but Albert forgot two important things. As I mentioned, if cocktails are your poison, you had better take your own ingredients and shaker to Nigeria. The reaction to Albert's highly Western idea could hardly be described as enthusiastic. A few weeks later he would make a similar mistake by offering a mattress as a reward to the winner of a game. For the rest of the series the mattress was left outside in the rain, until we decided to remove it from camera.

Albert also forgot that very few people can read a compass, much less know how to row. The participants' training consisted of fifteen minutes of "rowing". Most of them couldn't even stay afloat.

After the participants got into the canoes, they rowed around in circles. Not because they wanted to, but because it was all they could manage. There was no team effort, just a group of hyperactive individuals who splashed wildly on their own to get somewhere as quickly as possible. One canoe gravitated in the direction of Lagos and we had to head them off several times or this was where they'd have ended up. The other canoe headed off into the deep sea. It was as hilarious as Abbott and Costello's antics, but not the right kind of television viewing if you're looking for a national icon for Gulder.

Gulder's idea was that the 'last man standing' would be their ambassador for their beer for a year. From the word go it was clear that it would be a tough call. Those who were good-looking and had a body to match didn't have the intellectual capability to solve a basic riddle. The one or two who were sharp enough to solve a riddle were klutzes who fell over their own feet. But the one thing they could all do very well was argue.

Arguing is a national sport in Nigeria for which they'll win gold in the Olympic Games – no contest. For some reason the arguing never escalated to physical violence, even though Nigeria is a reasonably violent country. The fact that you can't apply for bail when you're awaiting trial might have something to do with it. There was a case of a guy who was arrested after he allegedly hit a policeman. Five years later he was found innocent but he still spent five years in prison.

When the participants were still on the mainland, they believed they would do a few activities each day and then return to their hotel at night to enjoy a hearty meal, watch a little television and bask in their new-found fame. When the programme presenter, my jolling partner Chidi, showed them where they had to build their camp on the island reality finally hit them.

We had ten very upset Nigerians on our hands. Their joy at eventually arriving on the island after hours of rowing and explanations off camera was soon forgotten. They had to go to work and build a shelter on an island where it rains every night. They started fighting with each other and by this I don't mean that they merely exchanged opinions. They shouted loudly and furiously at each other leaving no pause for possible rebuttal. It went on and on … and on, until they were physically exhausted. Only then did they build a sloppy shelter of sorts.

We had neither an Einstein nor a Charles Atlas, but at least we now knew that all the fighting would ensure a successful television programme.

Shooting on an underdeveloped and almost uninhabited island comes with a unique set of predicaments. Especially with a programme of this extent, which could easily become a logistical nightmare. Everything had to be brought to Snake Island by boat. This included generators and vehicles – literally every single thing we needed. If something broke it had to be taken back and repaired or a technician had to be brought from Lagos to fix it. In the process you could lose an entire day. And you can say what you like about Land Rovers – they do get stuck. A brand new one with less than 200 kilometres on the clock found its final resting place on the island – it's probably overgrown, rusted and stripped, but it's still there.

There was one other exceptional aspect about the *Gulder Ultimate Search*. And if you tell this fact to anyone who has ever worked on a reality television programme, watch the growing disbelief on their face: there would be an hour long episode every day. Usually each episode consists of a few days shooting and the clips are then joined to look like one day. In addition, we also had to deliver episodes for twenty-one consecutive days. Usually there is one episode a week. Lastly, to prevent news on the progress of the programme from leaking out each episode was broadcast two days after it had been recorded. The cutting and sound mixing therefore had to be done in one day in order to get a neatly finished programme ready for airing. That's a challenge few producers will accept.

This meant that for the duration of the shoot we also had to stay on the island. As the island didn't have any hotels, rondavels or other standard accommodation our office and sleeping quarters was the abandoned house of a Nigerian general. There was no running water, a problem that was never solved. The sleeping arrangements were haphazard to say the least. There were no beds. My bed was a foam rubber mattress 6 cm thick (I measured it), which had been placed on the ground without any covering. Anyone who has ever been in the tropics will tell you how important a bed with legs is if you want to avoid the nocturnal creepy crawlies.

Two people shared a room. Well, that is if you were one of the important people – like the six whiteys from South Africa (I'll tell you about the rest later). Albert snored like a pig and so did Femi, the voice artist. As luck would have it, they were both in the room next to mine and on the other side was the edit suite, which was a buzz of activity 24 hours a day so that we could meet our deadlines. I didn't have a desk in my room but crafty Taiwo, the art director, cut down a tree and made me one. You could only get cell phone reception if you climbed over the balcony railing and hung on by one arm rather like a monkey. We all shared one bathroom.

Clearly I was under the mistaken impression that we were there to make a reality television programme, not to be part of one. Oh, and someone forgot to tell the general that we were staying in his house, but we managed to overcome that minor problem later.

This was only the start of our logistical difficulties. After we left Lagos we not only lost contact with reality, we were also left to the tender mercies of good friends – such as the money thief Innocent and the bullfrog Bobby. A third person whose name I can't recall completed the gruesome threesome. She worked for an events company and was responsible for the logistics behind the shoot. It was soon clear that we would get the worst of it. The supply system sounded quite simple. This anonymous woman – let's call her Mercy, because that's the one thing she never showed us – Bobby and Innocent would get cash at the agency to buy food, water and other essentials for us.

The agency had no way of determining how the money was spent, because a lot of the essentials were bought on Lagos' streets without any cash slips. You don't need an imagination powered by rocket fuel to know where this story is heading. Mercy, Bobby and Innocent enriched themselves on a truly grand scale while we eked out a miserable existence on the island. Some days we didn't have any food, because the three musketeers stole too much. On other occasions our salaries were short. The excuse was that there weren't enough dollars available in Lagos. Any Nigerian would have a good laugh about that one. We were not amused. Our future depended on these three villains. Everyone, including the agency, knew what was happening, but simply accepted it as the price of doing business in Nigeria.

A few days into the shoot Brenda Fassie died on 9 May and on 10 May our co-director Lewis contracted malaria. Whether it was a cosmic turn of events, I'll never know, but it was fatal to lose one of your directors on a shoot of this magnitude.

At least Lewis had a room and a bed. The rest of the film crew's accommodations were slightly more primitive and unorthodox to say the least – three of them had to make do in a two man tent. That's where they could relax after working for twelve hours every day. The toilets were long drops. They brushed their teeth at one tap in the backyard.

The idea of a tropical island conjures up an image of something out of *Condé Naste Traveller.* Snake Island wasn't like that at all. The jungle was dense and we had the good fortune to arrive at the start of the rainy season. Lagos' average annual rainfall is 2500 mm. I think most of it came down in torrents when we were there. One thing that you can see clearly from Snake Island is an imminent storm. It was awe-inspiring. You saw the clouds over the sea hours before they reached the island, and they rolled and grumbled from about 100 kilometres away before they hit the island as a solid grey wall powered by fiery flashes of lightning. The sight of the palm trees bending over in the fierce wind to touch their toes was breath-taking, and every time a storm hit the island I'd get new respect for Mother Nature.

Rain or shine, the shoot had to carry on – one episode a day. It wasn't as if we could put the day on hold and carry on later. We had to press on and keep shooting. And in the stormy weather when we eventually got to our beds they were usually drenched.

The violent weather was nerve-racking. I've never thought that fear is a good thing, but I can't stand the sight of a storm, the lightening and thunder, the continuous downpour from a dark and ominous looking sky. All I wanted to do was cower away somewhere safe and dry. One of the storms that in my limited experience would rate as a contender for Tropical Storm of the Year was so bad that Kadaffi, a guy who weighs about 130kg and could easily play lock forward for the Bulls, was blown thirty metres away while in his tent. The rest of the guys who weren't in their tents at the time had a difficult job trying to find the pieces and put them back together. We had to commission one of the locals to climb up a palm tree to retrieve some of the remnants. As we didn't have any extra tents we used gaffer tape to stick them together and hoped they'd last for the rest for the rest of the shoot.

The chef slept on the concrete floor in the kitchen, until someone put his foot down and insisted that he be given a mattress. He got the mattress that was the discarded prize of one of the contestants.

During the storms the shoot deteriorated into total chaos as everyone simply tried to survive. Tempers flared and arguments broke out all over the show. The participants' chances of becoming heroes were starting to disappear fast. One night, during yet another severe downpour they decided enough was enough. There was a mutiny: they simply walked off the set, knocked on our door and insisted on going home.

When the participants in a reality television programme wake you in the dead of the night and tell you that they are done, you have a serious problem on your hands. Only after they were threatened that they would be held financially responsible for every single expense did they skulk back to their shelter.

Our set doctor, Dr Coco, brought a large supply of Valium back to the island after one of his trips to Lagos. Things were more peaceful from then on. I suspect he had been a keen user himself because he was the only one who smiled throughout the whole shebang.

Meanwhile the production manager, Jamie, kept on transgressing every written (and some unwritten) rules of what was socially acceptable. Even the normally patient Nigerians started to grumble. Jamie was the first one to go stir crazy in the jungle. Shortly afterwards he went home, because of some kind of illness, but we all knew Snake Island broke him. Years later he became a renowned celebrity chef on a popular international channel. That was more his cup of tea.

The rest of us were now living and looking more and more like wild people – to such an extent that the people from the agency no longer wanted to stay over for the night when they came to check up on us. They would arrive in the late afternoon to collect the broadcast tape and then leave rather suddenly under the pretence that they had other urgent matters to attend to. People were running scared of us. It was a *Lord of the Flies* situation. What happened behind the scenes would have made far better television viewing than what happened in front of the cameras.

Then tropical storm Dorette hit us. She was a late addition to the team after the local editors could not keep up with the work. We didn't get a forecast warning about her arrival or a forecast intensity for that matter – she was hastily flown in from South Africa to save the day.

Dorette immediately endeared herself by calling everyone together, including the director, producers, writer, voice artist and presenter, to inform us that we were messing things up, that she was going to take over and that we all had to listen to her. Even Dr. Coco's Valium couldn't prevent the unpleasant reactions to her little speech.

If Dorette had just been another overzealous editor, I could have handled the situation, but unfortunately I had a history with her. I was in my early thirties when my first marriage failed and I fell in love with Dorette, who was in matric at the time. It's not something I'm particularly proud of, but it happened. The only problem was that Dorette thought she was going to become the next Mrs Maas and I had other plans. When I married the second time, Dorette made a second appearance but this time it was like something out of *Fatal Attraction*. She delivered letters addressed to me at our house, sent text messages and made a right royal nuisance of herself. My wife didn't appreciate the attention and just the mention of her name caused confrontation. And now she was here in foreign parts, one bedroom away from me, and I didn't know how to tell my wife.

My decision to try the "if you ignore it, the problem will disappear" approach did not work. The news somehow reached South Africa that she was on set. A number of extremely disagreeable conversations between me and my dear wife ensued, which were aggravated by poor cell phone reception. Needless to say, it didn't help to smooth things over.

Before we bumped into each other in Nigeria Dorette had been in

London for a few years. It was during the rave explosion and South African manufactured disco biscuits (better known as ecstasy among those who don't use it) were a big hit. Ravers ate handfuls of the stuff because it supposedly didn't have any side-effects. Dorette might have had one or two too many because she wasn't the Dorette I knew from before. In fact, I thought I recognised the first signs of dementia.

In Johannesburg she was able to hide it from clients, but under the pressure of Snake Island it was impossible. She stayed up nights on end and edited the same thing over and over. She started talking incoherently and referred to things that never happened. She stopped washing her feet (just her feet) – this was always a bad sign. She started talking about the bodies buried under the house. And like an Ingrid Jonker copycat she walked into the sea to end it all.

It was blatantly obvious that Dorette would be the jungle's next victim and because she was my ex I was expected to look after her. The easiest solution was to break into the only other holiday home on the island, and hold her down on the bed while Dr Coco gave her an injection that knocked her out for 48 hours (with medication I had to pay for). She was then put on an aircraft home. Bobby stole the 1 000 dollars they still owed her.

At first I thought I was in *Fitzcarraldo*, but then I started to realise that I was in *Apocalypse Now*. If Joseph Conrad wrote his story on Snake Island, it would have been much darker.

Conversation with one of the Nigerian members of the crew:
"When you heard that you were going to be working with a bunch of white South Africans, what did you expect?"
"PW Botha."
"What did you get?"
"Mostly PW Botha, but some Mandelas, too."

The client continued to criticise the programme in every possible way and in hindsight he could have been right. However, under the circumstances it was the best we could do. And the viewers didn't mind that it wasn't technically perfect. During the broadcast the traffic in Lagos came to a standstill. Conversations in bars were dominated by the *Gulder Ultimate Search* and during the first week of broadcast Gulder's beer sales rocketed by 25%. We had a huge hit on our hands. Newspapers wrote endless articles and blogs went mad.

The popularity of the series resulted in one problem. The winner of the series had to discover a "treasure". The story I made up about the treasure was that a pirate was shipwrecked on Snake Island with a chest of gold tied to his hand. He buried the chest and nobody knew where the chest was. Each day the participants received a few clues through tasks and riddles that helped them to compile a map of where the treasure was buried.

Yeah, I know it's not my most original idea, but at the time it was the best I could come up with. And it worked. It worked so well that boatloads of guys with spades and metal detectors started arriving on the island in the hope of getting their hands on the fictitious treasure before the participants. Some were very unsavoury characters and things started to get a bit dangerous. One group of scoundrels even insinuated that we knew where the treasure was and that they had ways of getting us to talk that would not be a pleasant experience.

The solution was to send for reinforcements – more guys with AK47s. Some of them were also hoping to lay their hands on the treasure – and they were armed. We doubled-up the Valium.

Not that we weren't surrounded by enough disagreeable characters and I don't mean the usual ignoramuses such as the representatives from the agency and the client. From the outset we were warned not to go outside the protected terrain after nine at night, as it was dangerous. However, nobody wanted to tell us what the danger was.

Ibeshe, the town (I use the term loosely) closest to us was about a 20 minute walk away. The residents didn't have any visible sign of income. There were no maize fields or any other signs of agriculture. And yet all the young men on the island had expensive watches, smart clothes and the latest cell phones. Their boats, although somewhat battered, were equipped with the latest and most powerful outboard engines available.

Rumour had it that there was a small bar in Ibeshe, so late one afternoon I walked in that direction to swallow down some of my frustration with a cold beer. The London Town Pub had three clay walls, a rickety sign and a rusted corrugated lean-to supported by two palm trunks. The seats and tables were made of local wood. This should have been a clear warning, because the beer companies in Nigeria provide plastic tables and chairs with their trade mark to even their smallest clients. The London Town Pub was way off the grid.

The men in the bar had just got out of bed and my arrival wasn't exactly met with a fanfare. I sat down at a table and ordered a 600ml beer for R5. A party of investigators was immediately sent to my table by one of the older men who was clearly the leader of the pack. Where did I come from, who was I, what was I doing there ... all the usual questions.

At first I thought they could be pirates. Sometimes, when ships waited for weeks to dock in Lagos, they were attacked and robbed by guys in boats. The pirates usually didn't steal the load, but rather cash, cell phones, that kind of thing. Then I thought the men could be smugglers, because the island was on the main smuggling route from Benin. They usually smuggled materials, cigarettes and liquor to evade import tax. But these men were self-confident and their muscles flexed under their neat clothes.

Suddenly I knew in whose company I was: the famed "oil bunkerers" whom I'd read about at length before coming to Nigeria.

Crude oil is transported via pipeline to where it is loaded onto ships. These pipes are on the surface to make it easier to maintain them. Some go through towns but the residents never see any of the money from the oil. So they drill holes in the pipelines, steal the oil and sell it to corrupt ship captains. Of course, it was illegal, but so are many other things which happen in Nigeria.

It is extremely dangerous to be an "oil bunkerer", because you are targeted from three sides. If you are caught out by the police or the army, they take it very personally since they hate any form of competition. In Nigeria the death sentence still applies and although the government does not mete it out as generously as China, you don't have to be a murderer to lose your life.

Secondly, you could get ructions from other oil thieves, because every town near the pipeline has its own group of "oil bunkerers". Each group may only steal a certain quantity, or the oil company might suspect foul play and start investigations. If one group steals too much, it causes problems for all the towns along the route. Gang wars are regular occurrences when one group feels that another has stolen too much. And you'll remember that the AK47 is the way problems are solved here.

Lastly the oil thieves also got it in the neck from the oil companies who acted as though they were above the law. They have their own armies and aren't bashful about deploying them. During my unforgettable stay on Snake Island the government gave part of the island to a well known oil company. I won't mention the name of the oil company. The fact that the land had been inhabited by a group of people for generations didn't seem to bother the government or the oil company. The oil company simply sent in a bunch of mercenaries and invaded the area. The residents armed themselves and the result was a mini war – we heard the shots every night. Sometimes the oil companies gave up, usually when their financial advisors told them that the profit would not be large enough. Sometimes the local residents packed up and made a contribution to Lagos' unemployment problem. I don't know who won that particular fight.

My drinking pals in the bar were a bunch of adventurers with a short life expectancy. It was always fun hanging out with people like that. By nine o'clock I was ready to go back to my quarters, but my new friends insisted on showing me their dark secret. I suspect they wanted to impress the *oyibo*. The large quantity of beer, Johnny Walker and island dagga made it an easy decision.

The older man, the leader of the group, said that if I ever told anyone about what they were going to show me, he would cut off my head. He has passed on since; murdered by a younger guy who wanted to take over his position, so the promise I made to him is no longer valid. In the pitch dark they led me to a place on the island that I had not been to before. I was excited, because I was going to experience something I had only read about.

The area where the pipeline was situated was surrounded by warnings about quicksand. It was the only spot on the entire island where nothing grew and the one small sign of robust life was the mosquitoes. Within a few steps my shoes were filled with crude oil that could no longer sink into the sand.

It was a very basic operation. There was a pipeline with a deep hole dug underneath it. There was a plug that closed off a hole in the pipe. When they extracted the plug, the hole below the pipe filled up with oil and they baled out the oil with buckets. Later someone brought a generator with a pump, which accelerated the process. They poured the oil into large drums, loaded the boat and headed off into the sea to offload their cargo. I declined their offer to join them for the trip.

Nobody smoked. Quite a few of these guys had literally gone up in a puff of smoke during an explosion. They stopped working just before daybreak, as they considered it too dangerous to carry on with the skies getting lighter. I was a bit disappointed as I expected something slightly more thrilling, but I'm a take-it-as-it-comes kind of guy. While I walked away I wondered whether this primitive way of stealing oil could really hurt a large company financially. The answer is yes, but you can't help wondering how big the bunkerers' balls really were.

---

**"First reality TV show berths with Ultimate Search"**

Nigerian Breweries Plc is set to pioneer the country's first reality TV Show, tagged the *Gulder Ultimate Search*. The package, a live adventure series that will project the positive values of youth, intellect, strength, valour and courage is to be featured on selected TV stations in Nigeria and on DStv.

It is working in collaboration with a 6-man team of top TV producers from South Africa. Sources close to the team revealed that beside skilled manpower deployed for the show, sophisticated equipment has been acquired to provide a world class production support for the reality TV menu.

The show, which industry pundits have adjudged as the biggest and most exciting marketing campaign ever to take place in Nigeria, is to be shot on Snake Island for a period of 21 days.

*Vanguard*, March 2004

---

It was the start of a new day. And as usual in Nigeria, every day came with its unique challenges. So between the motorcycle that broke down on day one and the Land Rover that got stuck on day five, which no one could free from its sandy grave, we ended up walking much farther each day than any of the participants. They were also fed more regularly than we were. I started wondering whether they would have stayed on the island so peacefully if they knew about the chaos and mayhem behind the scenes and how often things nearly didn't come together.

Thirty to forty mosquito-bites a night was the going rate, we had to contend with sand-beetles and each morning we religiously did our malaria tests. The tropics don't exactly treat electronic equipment with kid gloves. We started out with fifteen cameras. On day 13 only eight still worked. The end was in sight. On day 14 the voice artist packed his bags because he had not been paid a cent. On day 15 the presenter packed his bags because he had not been paid either. His words to the client were: "My mind is confused. I cannot think. I can only think when I have been paid."

Suddenly they were paid, but my money was still outstanding. I decided to hide the master copy of the next broadcast tape until everyone on set was paid. On day 17 one of Bobby's slaves tried to steal the master copy from the edit suite. The edit suite was on the first floor and the stairs were guarded by one of our friends who carried an AK47. Bobby's slave then tried to get into the window with a rope. Somebody pushed him and he fell – suit and all – on his backside in the tropical mud.

We were paid.

On day 19 the production manager got jungle fever and typhoid. The same day someone from the agency came to see how it was going and experienced the anger first-hand. He didn't even visit the set; he just fled back to his boat with the words: "You all look like wild men."

The only thing left to tell in this story is the issue of the general's house, which was used as headquarters and hotel for the production of the *Gulder Ultimate Search* – without his consent. On day 20 we were informed that the general was on his way to see us. He had eventually heard about the situation and he wasn't impressed with the news. We couldn't even try to pull the wool over his eyes – there was no way that we could evacuate the place and hide the equipment and people in time. It was the second last day of the shoot and too many things were happening. Any plans for evacuation were aborted. Nobody cared what happened anyway. He could have arrived with his entire military force and no one would have given them a second look. We were beyond the point of caring. Not only did we look like "wild men", we also thought and acted like them. We were in a place where logic or reason did not exist. We were machines fighting for survival and not even a general was going to stand in our way.

Fortunately somebody high up realised what would happen if things went wrong. In the end the general never arrived. Rumour had it that he got a fat bribe to cancel his trip to the island. Like any solid Nigerian citizen he couldn't turn down a good offer.

On day 22 I was woken by the noise of the film crew busy packing up for the return journey to Lagos. The previous day had been our last day of shooting. Everything that was brought to the island during the past three weeks had to be carried to the beach and loaded onto small boats.

I had a thumping headache thanks to too much Gulder and Remy Martin. I had partied the night away with sixty other people who wanted to dance the past three weeks into oblivion. On an open-air dance floor with a solitary lamp as the only lighting we danced to Fela Kuti's afro beat. Here in the middle of a tropical jungle we sang with Fela and shared his pain and suffering, because we had experienced it first-hand.

The beer was protected by the two largest guys on set. They made sure everybody got their fair share of alcohol. The Remy Martin was a gift to Chidi, which he gladly shared with me.

A week later, during the public party to honour the winner, the agency made its final and most spectacular blunder. They advertised the *open party* on radio. If they still had any reservations about the popularity of the programme, the party cleared away their last doubts. People broke windows to get into the hall after they were refused entry at the door. In the streets thousands of people jostled each other to get in. Eventually the police had to use tear gas to disperse the crowd.

By that time I was long gone, back in South Africa and stuffing myself with all the scrumptious food and treats I'd had to go without during my adventure, and taking great pride in the fact that I'd withstood all the trials and tribulations Nigeria threw my way with inextinguishable valour.

# WITBOY'S TRAVEL TIPS

§   When, after two days of empty promises, you still don't have warm water in your hotel room in Lagos, I would suggest the following: go to reception dressed only in your underpants, throw one hell of a tantrum and tell them that the South African president will become personally involved if the problem isn't fixed right away. This method even works on a Sunday.

§   When someone carries an AK47 he is always right.
    When someone carries an AK47 he is always right except if you have American dollars.
    When you have American dollars, the guy with the AK47 is still in the right but he'll probably be a bit friendlier.

§   Never, ever, stay in room 203 in the City Lodge Hotel[9] in Jos, Nigeria. It has a view of the parking area where rowdy early-morning drivers kick up the kind of racket you only hear at Kyalami.

§   When a travel agent books you into a guesthouse in Harlem, New York, under the pretext that the neighbourhood has been gentrified, they are taking you for a ride. Harlem still looks like Hillbrow on New Year's Eve except that the American police are far more dangerous.

§   In Europe the girls like you because you're interesting; in the

---

9   This hotel has nothing to do with the South African chain, except the name, which its Nigerian owners stole.

USA they like you because you have an accent, and in Africa they like you because you have money.

§ Every hoodlum and hotel clerk (the two are often the same person) knows where tourists carry their money belts.

§ It's far less trouble to walk to Europe than to fly with Iberia, except if you're broke and under 25.

§ Don't allow Spanish customs officials to convince you that your white jacket will still be white when it emerges from the x-ray machine. They are lying.

§ Never underestimate legendary German precision. When the announcement board at a German train station says that the train will arrive at 12.23 it *always* does.

§ Avoid the Tourist Hotel at the station in Antwerp at all costs. You might just confuse it with a hotel in a war-torn African country when you wake up with an Absinthe hangover. It's more comfortable to sleep on the bench at a bus stop.

§ When you drink in the harbour in Antwerp, there is a strong possibility that you'll see someone's hacked-off head in a garbage bin. It will usually belong to a Russian sailor who owed someone money. For Pete's sake, do not get involved.

§ The Czech police are just as efficient and educated as their South African counterparts.

§ Forget about American tourists – drunken English soccer fans are a far greater threat to world peace.

§ When an "interesting old man" suddenly starts talking to you in a bar in Prague, chances are that his pal is busy stealing someone's camera or laptop.

§ Taxi drivers over the world are cultivated from the same gene in a laboratory.

§ Madagascar's beach towns do not have toilets. Not even for the residents. When you walk from the village to the sea, the ablution facilities for men are to the right and those for women to the left of the foot-path. This means that when you walk on a beach towards a town, be on the look out for deposits. It's not good manners to make eye contact with someone who is doing their business.

# REALITY TV: A RUDE AWAKENING
## Obudu, 2005

**T**HE *Gulder Ultimate Search* Part Deux started with the American rapper 50 Cent and a very important lesson he had to learn in Nigeria – Africa isn't for sissies.

This self-proclaimed low-life, who had been shot on many occasions, decided to honour Nigeria with his presence. A big concert was arranged for Lagos and another one for Port Harcourt, the main centre in an oil-rich area. Port Harcourt is the most rough-and-tumble city in Africa that isn't involved in a war. Kidnappings were a daily occurrence back in 2005 and the police had a tough job clearing away the bodies after the previous night's knifings and shootings.

50 Cent's concert in Lagos was such a runaway success that it almost justified the size of his ego and his diamond-encrusted, chain-wearing entourage. His posse consisted of the usual bunch of bad asses who carried illegal weapons and beat up young fans asking for 50 Cent's signature. You know, those salt-of-the-earth types that rappers like to hang out with. Men whose wayward behaviour was worth more on paper than in real life.

Now in Lagos you get these guys who call themselves "area boys". You could compare them to our tsotsis, only they are much more dangerous. As their name indicates, they control certain parts of the city and nothing happens there without their permission. They often operate like paramilitary units and in some cases even have important political contacts. The area boys are strong, ruthless and not in the least bit afraid to use violence to get their own way. It's tough to grow up poor and on the streets in Lagos – it's far worse than anything you would experience in Queens, New York, where 50 Cent's posse came from.

The musician Eedris Abdulkarim, who was the opening act for 50 Cent, was a hero of the area boys. He boasts that he himself was once an area boy, but today he is one of the most popular rappers in Nigeria. He wears his crime record with the same pride that an African dictator wears his (fake) medals. What sets Eedris apart even more is the fact that he grew up a Muslim in a predominantly Christian city where tolerance among religious groups did not feature high on the agenda.

In any other country being the opening act for a big American star like 50 Cent would be a good thing. But no, not in Nigeria where megalomania takes on a totally new meaning. I doubt if we'll ever know exactly what happened in the dressing room before the concert in Lagos, but what happened after that altercation became one of the juiciest pieces of gossip in a long time. It was the first thing I heard when I got off the plane at the Murtalla Mohammed airport in June 2005.

After the concert both artists and their parties had to fly to Port Harcourt in the same aircraft. Eedris and his henchmen were supposed to fly economy class, while 50 Cent and his troubadours would naturally fly first class. Eedris, however, decided that this wasn't good enough and promptly annexed 50 Cent's seats. When the American arrived, he had two options: He could either resign himself to a two-hour long flight with much less leg room than he was used to or he could fight to get back his seat in first class. He naturally chose to stand his ground, but he and his cronies got a serious beating in the ensuing scuffle.

Eedris and his men humiliated the American and his group to such an extent that they had to flee to their Hummer on the runway, lock the door from the inside and sit there for hours while they waited for their flight back to Atlanta. The Port Harcourt concert was cancelled and Eedris celebrated his victory by downing the entire stock of liquor in first class while he waited for the police to come and get him. In their infinite wisdom the police decided to wait until he finished his drinking binge and surrendered himself.

Only one American newspaper, the *New York Post*, picked up on the story, but 50 Cent and his team refused to comment. To add insult to injury Eedris later wrote a song about the face-off, which reached number one on every radio station in Nigeria. After he made a lot of money from the song, he impudently offered 50 Cent an official apology. Whether 50 Cent accepted his apology is unknown.

The Nigerians are a proud people and they like to describe themselves as The Giant of Africa. This term was first coined in the 1970s and they stubbornly still believe it even though it's often contradicted in reality. But events such as 50 Cent's bloody nose and bruised ego validate Nigerians' feelings of superiority.

Little did I know that the 50 Cent incident would be a prelude to what awaited me on my second visit to the country. I, too, would get a firsthand taste of at least one Nigerian's overinflated sense of self.

My home away from home in Lagos during the pre-production of the *Gulder Ultimate Search* (let's just call it the *GUS*) was the Hotel Support, which was ironically more of a burden than anything else. Where do I start? The air-conditioning was out of order, an absolute disaster in Lagos. From the heavily rusted water pipes burst forth a stream of water that looked like Coca-Cola complete with foam and unidentified floating objects. The hotel's cockroaches waged a reign of terror – entirely Baygon-resistant. They were so brazen that one night they devoured an entire packet of biscuits while I was sleeping.

And little did I know what awaited me in the breakfast room one morning. I inadvertently nearly caused a civil war by asking for a slice of cheese on my poached egg. The waiter, as always very attentive because he knew the *oyibos* tipped well, said he'd arrange it, no problem. But after a while I became aware of a big palaver in the kitchen. The voices became louder and more agitated and it sounded like pots and pans were being thrown around. Then I heard a few thumps as if someone was being punched. I could only assume that one of the waiters had slept with the chef's wife or girlfriend or something like that and continued to wait patiently for my poached egg and cheese.

When my egg on toast finally did arrive, it came without cheese. The waiter's propeller-like bow tie looked like it had been through a serious windstorm. He was dishevelled and very apologetic: Sorry, he said, but he couldn't add the cheese because they didn't know what it cost. Cheese wasn't listed as a separate item on the menu and no one could decide how much to charge me for it ...

By this time my cheese had become a matter of national importance. The hotel manager, who had been safely ensconced in his office during the commotion, now decided to enter the fray and even the clerk at reception came round to give his view on the matter. Everyone talked at once and the Yoruba flew left and right, as well as some spit (which luckily did not land on my egg).

So there I was, busy with my breakfast, which should have been a peaceful affair, while a chef in full regalia waved about a spatula, a clerk grumbled in my ears and the hotel manager tried to assert his authority. I'm not exactly a morning person, so I did what needed to be done.

"SHUT THE FUCK UP!" I shouted. Everybody froze. It probably wasn't the aggression in my voice, but the f-word that did the trick.

It was not often heard among this religious bunch who preferred to keep their sins secret.

"Gentlemen," I continued in the calmest of tones, "I'm sorry to have to tell you that I have changed my mind. I have decided I do not want cheese with my egg."

But even that did not stop the fighting. Long after I finished my breakfast the bellowing in the kitchen continued.

One of the things I learnt very quickly in Nigeria is that your position in the social pecking order is of extreme importance and you should know your place. The waiter reckoned he was entitled to decide what the cheese should cost because he had promised me the cheese. The chef felt his authority as head of the kitchen was being challenged because he wasn't consulted. The manager was simply a first-rate idiot who thought everyone had to listen to him. The moment someone challenged the line of authority the problems started.

Fortunately the Hotel Support and I soon parted ways. It wasn't a sad farewell. Tips for surviving your stay at the Hotel Support: Avoid Room 302 at all cost. And remember: if you meet someone by the name of Candice, immediately return to your room and lock the door, because you will not get rid of her. If she keeps on knocking, pretend you're asleep. If she gets the hotel manager to open the door with a master key, put a chair under the door handle. And if that still don't work, push a N500 note underneath the door. That usually worked.

The destination for *GUS 2* was the town of Obudu in the southeast of Nigeria on the border of Cameroon. To get there, you fly to Calabar and then brace yourself for a five-hour drive to Obudu. But it was already a big improvement on Snake Island. Even the Protea Hotel there could nearly live up to its South African counterpart.

The flight to Calabar, like any domestic flight in Nigeria, came with its unique set of challenges. Passenger safety wasn't exactly high on the priority list for the Federal Airports Authority of Nigeria (opportunely abbreviated to FAAN). Since 1969 there were more than sixty commercial flight accidents, and in most cases everyone on board died.

One of the reasons for the high accident rate could be that every Tom, Dick and Harry was allowed to start an airline. Nigeria's national carrier had been closed by the government for ages. It offered entrepreneurs the opportunity to start fly-by-night airlines, like the one we were to fly with. It's a very simple thing to start an airline: all you have to do is steal enough money if you are governor of one of the thirty-six states, bribe your friends in government to give you a license, buy a few aircraft and Bob's your uncle. There is one other important requirement: you must use the aeroplanes until they fall apart; that is, if they don't first fall out of the sky.

Domestic flights weren't computerised and each boarding pass was written by hand. So booking in a film crew of about 100 people took quite some time. On top of that Nigerians can't really be bothered by time or being punctual. They tend to report for a flight, but then go to visit friends outside the airport building. A flight could easily be delayed for two hours while you wear through the seat of your trousers on a small uncomfortable chair in a packed departure hall without air-conditioning. One of my friends once spent two days at the Lagos airport when a minister's wife hijacked their flight for a shopping trip to Paris.

To prevent luggage from having to be off-loaded when a passenger doesn't pitch in time, the luggage is stacked on the runway. Come wind, sunshine or rain, you have to queue with all the other passengers, point out your bags and check that it's loaded. If your luggage goes missing in Nigeria, it is lost forever. Lost and Found doesn't exist and if it did, the room would be empty.

Our unwilling air hostess handed me a hard biscuit and a cup of sweet tea without me even asking for it. Next to me sat a man who brought along his own companion: a live chicken whose feet were tied together. I fed my biscuit to the traumatised chicken. The man smelled of old sweat and his nails were dirty. I was stunned by the large gold ring on his one finger.

Two weeks later the same aircraft we had been on dropped like a stone – all 117 passengers died in the crash. The former president, Olusegun Obasanjo, announced a mourning period of three days – probably to make sure nobody rose from the dead. A few months later 96 people died when another aircraft from the same airline crashed. A year later 149 died in another accident. When the owner of the airline ran out of favours, his license was eventually revoked. Today his deserted aircrafts are rusting at airports across the country.

When I landed in Calabar it was my first time outside Lagos. It reminded me of Pietermaritzburg because of the broad streets with high trees and the old buildings, which were reasonably well maintained. One had the feeling that history was valued in this city. Calabar is the capital of the state Cross River, which got its name from the large number of rivers that join in this province and empty into the sea as a huge water mass. Calabar lies on the Calabar River, about eight kilometres from where all the rivers join up. The city has been an important trade centre since the colonial era.

There were definite efforts to market Calabar as a tourist destination. Although I wouldn't take my family there on holiday yet, there were signs of a revival. For the first time I experienced a kind of peacefulness in Nigeria. People went out of their way to treat you like royalty. The governor of the state, Donald Duke, was a bit of a phenomenon in Nigerian politics: an honest man – well, as honest as a politician can be. He soon realised that GUS would give him free publicity and he was therefore friendly and accommodating. He even made a contribution to increase the prize money.

But despite efforts to be more tourist friendly, the Metropolitan Hotel's lift did not work and I had to carry six weeks' luggage up six flights of stairs. The water was brown, the meat in the hotel's restaurant was burnt to a crisp (like everywhere in Nigeria) and the internet connection was powered by a steam locomotive. My room didn't look like the one on the hotel's website and surprise, surprise, they were overbooked, so I had to share a room. It only had one double bed. I don't like sharing a hotel room with someone who's not my life partner and I definitely don't share a bed with another man. It doesn't have anything to do with homophobia; it's all about my need for personal space.

At least in Calabar I was allowed to ride on an *okada*. As an *oyibo* in Nigeria you are always overprotected. I could understand that in the days of military dictatorships the government had to keep an eye on white people because they could have been spies for the CIA, but now it was for a slightly excessive fear of them being kidnapped. Almost everywhere I worked in Nigeria I was watched like a hawk and someone always knew where I was. I wasn't allowed to move around on my own and always had to have a police escort, especially in small towns.

The police escort meant that I travelled in a convoy in the middle vehicle. In front and behind of us was a black double-cab bakkie with blue lights and deafening sirens. The head of security for *GUS* sat on the right hand side in the passenger seat (in Nigeria they drive on the wrong side of the road, the only former British colony that does so) in the front bakkie. He was accompanied by a policeman who was armed with (yes, by now you know) … an AK47. On the back of the front bakkie there were another two policemen and the bakkie behind us carried four more guys with AK47s.

That was the best way to get attention. If you went to the expat shops in the larger towns, guards surrounded the shop, made sure there weren't any kidnappers inside and waited until you had finished your shopping. Your bag of groceries often cost more than their monthly salary.

All this fuss didn't make me feel special; it was the way things were done. Year after year my lamenting and sighing about the excessive protection fell on deaf ears and later I had to accept it gracefully.

Calabar was more rural and calm and fortunately, the safety team was also more relaxed. Since the moment I saw an *okada* for the first time in Lagos, I had wanted to hitch a ride on one. The idea of weaving through the murderous traffic without wearing a crash helmet and knowing that something could go wrong at any minute appealed greatly to my rebellious nature. The wind in my face made me smile broadly. There were quite a few things to see and do in Calabar and I decided to make the most of the day we stayed over.

About 30% of all slave trade in West Africa took place from Calabar. There were the usual, depressing slave related sights that are so popular with black American tourists. This day was no exception. Their loud voices echoed in the small underground, windowless rooms where so many people were removed from their loved ones and where some had died. The silent witnesses were the rusted chains and leg irons. More than two centuries after slavery was abolished the place still smelled of fear. I had to get out of there.

I understand that it's important to remember the past and that history will (hopefully) teach us not to repeat our mistakes. But I also believe that we don't necessarily need to be exposed to all the remnants from the past like the gloomy slave quarters in Calabar and the mountain of skulls in Rwanda.

On a more positive note I found out that the first Nigerian world boxing champion, Hogan "Kid" Bassey, hailed from a town just outside Calabar. And the Scotch missionary Mary Slessor made Calabar her base at the end of 1800s and started a campaign against the custom of killing twins and their mothers at birth. The area has the highest incidence of twin births in the world. Slessor also campaigned for women's rights, because the average Nigerian woman wasn't and to this day isn't exactly treated like a queen.

The state Cross River has three main languages: Efik, Ejagham and Bekwara, but another fifty languages are spoken here. Not dialects – individual languages. It is also widely believed that the areas surrounding Calabar contain the world's largest diversity of butterflies, a handful of endangered gorillas and the last rain forest left in Nigeria. There is an almost romantic aura around rain forests when you read about them or watch a television programme on them. But to shoot a television programme in one is pure hell as I was to find out a day or two later.

One of the weirdest things in Calabar must have been the By the Grace of God Fattening Clinic. After we passed it I persuaded the *okada* driver with an extra N100 to turn around and go back so that I could find out more. The Fattening Clinic was meant for exactly what its name said. Ordinarily men weren't allowed at the clinic and although the proprietress was initially hesitant to share any information with me, I managed to charm her with my cute smile.

The treatment at the clinic was called *nkuho* and was peculiar to Calabar. Although it wasn't quite as bad as making *foie gras* it boiled down to more or less the same thing. Women were fed porridge and other starches up to seven times a day. While brides in the rest of the world try to be as slim as possible for their wedding day, the Nigerians in the east of their country put a 180 degree spin on that idea. Here it was a disgrace to be thin on your wedding day, because it implied that you were too poor to buy food. If you were single, it was acceptable and even preferable to be skinny, but when you got married you had to be plump, or better still, fat.

The proprietress described the treatment as "an instrument of empowerment and fertility control" for women. According to her men liked thin girls when they were on the prowl, but when they married they wanted a "real" woman. She had to look like an earth mother, a fertile goddess who looked capable and willing to bear many children. When they were fat, women allegedly had the authority of a matriarch and their relationships with their husbands were much stronger.

I didn't want to get involved in a protracted discussion, but I felt obliged to point out at least two contentious points in her argument. Firstly, the fattening up actually disempowered a woman, because her husband would satisfy his thin-fetish elsewhere while she was preparing food at home. Secondly, it was a clever way to ensure that your wife was unattractive to the men who do have an obsession with thin women.

Of course I was being critical, but somehow the proprietress thought that I had complimented the treatment. She even said that if the treatment had the benefits that I had just pointed out, it would by a very good thing. We were obviously standing on different sides of the Niger delta.

The Fattening Clinic wasn't a cheap place to seek assistance in this weighty issue and her clients were among the rich of Calabar. Apparently there were cheaper versions of the clinic where the poorer and rural people went. They also offered other services like obedience training for the brides-to-be. Usually the brides went to the clinic about two weeks before the wedding. Oddly enough the proprietress didn't understand what I was getting at when I asked her when the measurements for the wedding dress were taken.

My day in Calabar was at an end. We had to embark on our long journey to Obudu, but my stomach was already in a knot. The memories of the hardship on Snake Island were still all too fresh in my memory.

Seen on the road between Calabar and Obudu:
- An outdoor advertisement for a church with a large photograph of a Mercedes Benz and the words: "God is not moved by what you drive, but by what drives you." The photograph was lifted from the internet, because it was entirely pixelated.

- Names of shops: God Time is the Best Time Hair Salon, White Soul Motors, The Lord's Furniture Store, Final Home (a place that manufactured coffins) and billboards for Dry Bones Shall Rise Again Charismatic Church Services and the Lose Your Womb Fertility Crusade.

- Garages with no petrol.

- Trees with leaves larger than both of former Springbok Frik du Preez's hands.

- "Forest": A sign in the middle of a forest so dense that the trees form a canopy across the road and you drive in a natural tunnel for kilometres.

- Flowers as large as church bells that even look like church bells.

- Broken down trucks simply abandoned next to the road waiting to be claimed by the jungle.

- The word "NAAI" (Nigerian Achievers Award Institute) painted onto an official government vehicle.

- An advertisement board with this bold piece of wisdom: "Don't trust a woman."

In Nigeria there is a minute difference between a vehicle that qualifies as roadworthy and one that is unroadworthy. I suspect the traffic police will only declare your vehicle unroadworthy when the hooter is out of order. It was also like travelling through a maze of mobile Bible verses as most cars, buses and taxis had a verse painted or printed on them. Some were stickers and others were hand-painted works of art.

After you spent some time on the road, you realised why it was expedient to leave your fate to a Higher Hand. It's difficult to describe a car journey in Nigeria to someone who hasn't experienced it for themselves. Especially when the sidewalk suddenly becomes an extra lane. It's like unprotected sex: dangerous and exciting, but something you have to experience to know what it is all about. I have a strong suspicion that if you really mess up in this life you'll be reincarnated as a driver in Nigeria.

Things like a police truck with blaring sirens and the sound of a Jim Reeves' cassette played over and over weren't factors that made the trip to Obudu any easier. The journey lasted five fatiguing hours. Our arrival in Obudu with the security team's sirens going full-blast immediately focused the attention on us, something we specifically asked should not happen. The series was going to be difficult enough to shoot and we didn't want the locals to know too much about us. Well, that particular wish wasn't going to come true.

Obudu was your standard Nigerian town. Everything was a uniform brown – starting with the rusted corrugated huts where telephone cards were sold to the surrounding mud huts. It was as if nothing was allowed to have any colour – even the brightly-coloured material sold on the market soon faded after it was washed in the local water. Obudu had no historical value. It was just a town in the middle of nowhere where the residents were forced to survive.

A small shop that stocked Western groceries was cramped and all its merchandise was covered by a layer of dust. It was clear that there was little need or money for these products. Most of the items were past their sell by date by more than two years and the packet of biscuits I bought was musty.

To get to the set from Obudu was something else. Just outside Obudu there was a massive hill, about 1 500 metres above sea level, which towered above the surrounding landscape. The road up the hill was made up of eleven kilometres of sharp hairpin bends – one lane only. The road had such a steep incline that the production vehicle's brakes once caught fire on the way down. And this was the very spot where we had to shoot the second series – and also stay.

The difference in temperature between Obudu and the top of the hill was 15°C. In the next few weeks all of us who shuttled to and fro between the hill and the town caught colds and I contracted pneumonia.

Our hotel on the hill only looked good from the outside. But after our sojourn on Snake Island it would be hard to imagine worse accommodation. The fact that each of us had our own room with a television that worked most of the time scored major bonus points in my book. On the downside our hotel also didn't have bath plugs and warm water was a scarce commodity.

There was no electricity and the few generators that worked intermittently provided the power. A small generator ensured that we could do the normal 24-hour-day edits. The system remained the same: what was shot today was broadcast three days later. The only difference was that Lagos was now a five-hour trip and a two-hour flight away. It was a logistical nightmare, and I was truly thankful it wasn't my problem. There was a go-to guy whose only job was to move between the two points to deliver the tapes. Unfortunately, the Nigerian airline did not have a frequent flyer programme to reward him for his efforts.

One of the elements that make a reality television programme a success is the specific mixture of personalities who take part in it. Of course participants were chosen with this in mind. It's not the action that makes programmes like this work and become popular, it's the soapy element. This was where my work as writer and psychological manipulator came into play. The participants were chosen to reflect a variety of backgrounds, like the well-educated girl from a good home in Victoria Island (their version of Sandton) who felt strongly about women's rights, and stood against the typical chauvinist. Or the guy from a small town that put stock in traditional values and

had little education, who stood in stark contrast against the sophisticated global citizen.

I mastered the art of making quick deductions about who irritated
whom and then exploited the situation. At Obudu my nickname
among the participants was Triple-D – Deon De Devil. My role
was to pit participants against each other and send the programme
in a certain direction by using the information that I got in my daily
interviews with them. I tried hard to elicit reactions and cause
some stress among team members. The result hopefully made for
exciting viewing.

Sometimes it was easier said than done. The Nigerian society,
like any other, has its rules and norms. Each time the men built the
shelter when they arrived at the camp and the women cooked. The
thing was that it took a day or two at most to build the shelter, while
the women had to cook up to three times a day for the duration of
the series – 21 days. And while they slaved away behind the pots the
men would sit around and *gist* (the Nigerian word for talking shit).

It bothered me, but somehow not the female contestants. When
I asked them about it, they were quick to respond that this was how
things worked in their culture.

Then the puppet master started to play: You say you understand
their culture, but then wonder if they don't usually just cook for the
men close to them, like fathers, brothers and friends. When they nod
assent you point out that in this case they're cooking for men who are
in direct competition with them. Give them a few seconds to digest
this and you'll see on their faces how their hearts sink as they click.

The next day all the women were on strike. Suddenly they called
the male contestants lazy good-for-nothings and they insisted that
it was the men's turn to cook.

Now *this* is the role of a psychological manipulator.

To the same extent that we played mind games with the contestants,
the programme played its own cruel game with our production team.

When you work on set 24 hours a day without any of the ordinary duties like cooking, washing clothes and paying telephone bills you go into a different space. When you combine this with playing master manipulator the whole day, it places pressure on certain aspects of your life such as your relationships. Irrespective how solid they were, how communication was improved and how many ways there were to keep in contact with people, it caused problems.

Every single person on set, even the Nigerians who were only a few hours away from home struggled to keep marriages and relationships together. My and Pauli's problems usually started about a week after I left home. At first everything was hunky-dory, and then everything went haywire. My emotions went on a personal roller-coaster ride.

Suddenly you find that you share relationship issues with someone you barely know, just because you realise that they're experiencing the same problems. One of the benefits of this particular hotel was that it had a bar with a fireplace. For the first time there was a place where we could all hang out and talk about our problems. Usually relationships were high on the discussion list.

The *Gulder Ultimate Search 2* came with a very peculiar character. His name was Vaughn and he called himself The General. With slightly more power Vaughn would have made the perfect dictator. He was loud and overbearing and his suggestions were always right. He started each morning with a sermon: He stood up like a charismatic preacher and told everyone who wanted to hear (and those who did not) that women were lowly creatures not even worthy of licking a man's shoes. The General also regularly lost his cool and intimidated people.

That's not who he really was but for the first time we had someone on the programme who knew how to get the viewers' attention. The newspapers wrote about him endlessly and the internet chat rooms buzzed. People watched the programme to see what lunacy he would resort to next. He went on such tirades that he literally foamed at the mouth. Today The General is a very successful Nollywood actor who is cast in the same role over and over again.

Although his crazy behaviour made for riveting viewing there was one problem. Nigerian Breweries, who produced *Gulder,* were not interested in having such a controversial spokesman for their product. They felt he would damage the product's and company's image because he did not represent the trademark's values.

Under normal circumstances it would have been relatively easy to get rid of a contestant. Each person had his or her weakness and a good director knew what that was. If the client felt that a contestant was no longer suitable for the programme, the director quickly thought up a scheme to get rid of him. Some people can run far, some had the stamina to carry around heavy stuff, others could solve riddles easily ... There was one slight problem: Vaughn could do everything better than the other contestants. Irrespective of what we threw at him, he simply bounced back.

Not only did Vaughn know that he was the strongest, fastest and cleverest of the lot, he also knew we were trying to get rid of him. It soon developed into a full-blown cat and mouse game where Vaughn's resolve to stay in the game grew stronger each day.

The beer industry is ruthless. The previous year the raunchy Maritz was fired and everybody was holding their breath to see who would be the new victim. It was part of our reality behind the scenes. This year it was Oche's turn, the Nigerian Breweries' representative, but he asked for it. Oche kicked members of the production team out of their hotel rooms and rented them out to pocket the money. He used the rooms for his personal harem after he made a lot of empty promises to would-be female contestants about their participation in the show or how he could organise jobs for them at Nigerian Breweries.

It also was Oche's job to get rid of Vaughn. As time passed the pressure from Lagos increased to get Vaughn out of the programme. Our director, Lewis, and I were torn between our promise to produce good viewing and to meet the client's requirements. Eventually the producers came up with a full-proof plan. It would work and it wasn't even an excessively cunning plan: Vaughn was so unpopular among his fellow contestants, especially those who'd already been kicked out that we decided to bring them back for one night to choose someone who had to be kicked out … But the viewers' reaction was so overwhelming that we got a call from Lagos in the dead of night to say that we had to reinstate Vaughn onto the programme. We refused. The relationship between the big bosses and the production crew was now like a pressure cooker building up some serious steam.

Although our physical environment posed many challenges to the production team, this time the biggest problems started in the edit suites. This was where the big shots moved their attention. They chose their fighting ground well as it was much easier to interfere in the editing than on the set as the edit suite was in the hotel. Not only did the guys from the advertising company demand to give their opinion on how the story had to be told, the client also wanted to put his stamp of approval on the programme.

The thing that ripped the pressure cooker's sealing gasket right off came in the form of Kayode. He represented the advertising company and was the guy who would lose his job if the client's wishes were not met. It's a surprising fact that Nigeria has never had a rugby team. It isn't as if their men are puny. Even compared to his fellow countrymen Kayode was a giant. He weighed 130 kilograms and stood more than two metres in his socks. He had a booming voice, which could quieten the entire set in one second. He carried three cell phones and two two-way radios with him. Nothing happened without Kayode knowing about it.

Kayode and I began to have differing opinions on how "reality" should go down on the show. Instead of discussing things with me, he went behind my back to the editors and changed my stories. I don't suffer traitors gladly, but I grasped why the editors who were my subordinates were torn between following Kayode's instructions and going against mine. After the series I would return to South Africa, but there was a chance of getting more work from Kayode in the future if they complied with his requests.

My game plan changed to quiet, peaceful negotiation. Kayode was under pressure from Lagos to deliver a certain product and as someone who had worked in the corporate world for decades, I understood the position he was in. I hoped to reach a compromise, but Kayode wasn't interested. I then asked the director to issue an instruction to the effect that no changes could be made to any edit without our consent and on set the director's word is final.

The next day I was called in by the editors from the set at short notice. Kayode was pacing around the edit suite like a lion in a cage. He had two cell phone conversations on the go and was holding a third conversation with one of the editors. The moment he saw me he totally lost it and started shouting. Around us you could hear a pin drop. Two security guards with AK47s stormed in. A bloodbath was on the cards.

Kayode had one thing in mind – to show us once and for all who was the boss. By chance I had exactly the same plan, even though I only came up to his nipples. I could feel his rage. His entire body shivered. My knees shook, but I knew that if I displayed any sign of weakness I would never have the respect of the team again. I decided I had nothing to lose and started taunting him to hit me. At the same time I tried to remember whether I had informed Discovery that I'd left the country and whether they had a helicopter service – because there was no way Obudu's local hospital would be able to make me as good as new after Kayode had finished with me.

Then Kayode came at me. But before he could land his first shot, five people tackled him. For a non-rugby playing country the tackle was impressive. Four more people came to help and he was removed from the edit suite ranting and raving. I went to the bar to buy a bottle of cognac, which I emptied in long swigs next to a river. Somewhere in the middle of the night I woke up and stumbled back to the hotel. Meanwhile the hotel was on high alert because no one could find me. The next morning I had pneumonia.

Strangely enough, if you get pneumonia in Nigeria you get treated like a rock star. Because of the climate few people ever suffer from it. I had my own doctor and a nurse who looked in on me every 30 minutes to see whether I was still breathing and if I had a heartbeat. The doctor wrote a dissertation about my case because it was the first time he had had the opportunity to treat pneumonia.

My food was put in front of my bed and people knocked on my door softly and politely. They respected the small white laaitie who proved he had balls. Three days later when I was back on my feet the production team treated me like royalty. After that episode I never had a single problem with anyone on set.

Three days later I received my payment in a large brown envelope. The series was finished and it was time to go home.

### "Cult members beheaded student in Edo"

A final-year student of the College of Education was beheaded in a new dimension to the gory cult clashes that have nearly grounded academic activities in most tertiary institutions in Edo State. His remains were roasted while his skull was hung at the school gate.

Osawe Igbineoba was kidnapped on Saturday evening in the wake of renewed battles between rival cults. He was taken to an unknown destination where he was tortured to death before being beheaded and roasted. An employee of the college, who sought anonymity, said: "It was a gory sight on Monday morning to see the head of the abducted student already roasted and neatly delivered at the gate of the college."

*This Day*, May 2005

By this time I started to understand the subtler aspects of the Nigerian society better, but the way the cults were run still baffled me, as did certain of the animist activities. The term cult is usually used to describe an obscure and obsessive religious group, but it has a slightly different meaning in Nigeria. There the word cult is used to describe something similar to a gang. Unlike the gangs we're familiar with from the townships and the Cape Flats these gangs are active on campuses. This phenomenon is the Nigerian version of the American sorority system. The result is gang fights very similar to those in *West Side Story*.

It was a gory sight yesterday in Awka after the Anambra State Police Command raided some shrines in Okija in Ihiala local government area where they recovered 20 human skulls and one fresh dead body in a coffin. Thirty suspects were also arrested including the priests of two of the shrines.

The raided shrines included the dreaded Ogwugwu Isiula. The State Police Commissioner, Mr Felix Ogbaudu, who personally visited some of the shrines located in thick forests, said he counted about 50 corpses, some still fresh and headless ...

Though the priest of one of the shrines claimed that the skulls and the dead bodies were deposited by their owners because they were killed by the shrine by which name they swore to an oath, a native of Okija who tipped off the police, said the people were actually killed by the priests. He alleged that the priests killed their victims through what he called isusu and then ate them. He said the practice had existed for years but nobody was courageous enough to expose the perpetrators. He said he, however, took an oath with one of the priests for him to be able to penetrate the cult and have a first-hand knowledge of their mode of operation.

"We saw over 50 corpses in different stages of decomposition. People dying under questionable circumstances, they throw them into what I call 'evil forest'. Some of the bodies did not decompose, they kept shrinking. We are all aware that Okija is notorious for this kind of evil shrines in Igboland."

However, Secretary-General of Ohanaeze Ndigbo, Chief Joe Achuzia, yesterday took exception to the police raid of the two shrines in Okija, describing the action of the police as "ridiculous". The Ohanaeze scribe, who spoke on the development, decried the interest generated by the raid, saying worshipping at shrines was not new in Nigerian tradition. He said the issue portrayed the Igbo as cannibals, alleging that the police were out to rubbish the Igbo.

Achuzia recalled the history of the Okija shrine, saying it has a reputation for justice in the settlement of disputes among people, stressing that never in Igboland had anybody complained that the priests at the place killed or sacrificed human beings unjustly.

Said he: "Nobody has said that they kill people there. Those who go there, go there to settle their matters. They take oaths and at the end of the day, any of those found guilty is killed by the shrine. But it is obvious that not all cases are taken to this shrine because it is very powerful. The human parts and skulls which they discovered are merely those who had sworn at the place and apparently found guilty were killed not by any human being but the gods. Their bodies are usually brought to the place as sacrifice to the gods."

*- Vanguard*, May 2005

If you had to read this excerpt twice to make sure you caught everything, just one last comment: What struck me most about this bizarre newspaper article is that some of the bodies did not decompose, but dried out like mummies. You could, like me, question the existence of such voodoo or juju. What really made my hackles rise was the official who calmly admitted that people did die (or were killed) at the altar but then wondered why people had a problem with it.

These places of worship apparently provided a unique way of solving problems. If two people had a problem with each other, they went to the priest. They were convinced that the shrine would decide who was right or wrong and the one who was wrong would fall down dead. As was the case with the penis thefts, people strongly believed in the practice and if you believe so strongly in something it's easy to see the "signs" all around you.

It was widely believed that when the king of a tribe died the new king had to eat a piece of his heart. This ensured that tribal knowledge and the former king's power would be transferred to the new king's reign. Many maize fields were protected by small juju boxes, which prevented people from stealing your mealies. If you stole mealies, according to the tale, you would drop down dead.

Black magic abounded in Nigeria. There were always rumours of political leaders and prominent businessmen who believed various rituals would ensure they retained their power and prosperity. City dwellers, although they didn't often take part in rituals or even believe them, were nevertheless very wary of the guys who did believe in them.

# THE CHIEF AND THE YAM

Jos, 2007

Construction of the Sheraton in Jos was never completed because the state of Plateau got a new governor during the construction. When he suddenly demanded more money to give his approval to the project, the contractors decided that it was no longer financially viable to continue. The Sheraton's skeleton is like a monument to Nigerian corruption – and it has a breathtaking view over a lake.

Of all Nigerian cities Jos must have the most temperate climate. This means that more expats live here than in other parts and it's popular among the missionaries who don't want to sacrifice too much. It's situated in the high-lying part of Nigeria and is therefore also a popular place for athletes to train for competitions. The maize fields outside the city are surrounded by cacti that serve as natural protection again the harmattan, the desert wind that blows in from the Sahara over the region in January and dries out everything it its path. This is where the Nok, Nigeria's aborigines, first settled.

On paper Jos looked like an idyllic place where you could escape from the heat and madness of the other towns. As you know by now not everything in Nigeria is as it's supposed to be. The local airport was like stumbling onto a porn magazine with photographs of your grandma in it. All in all as classy as papsak wine. The drinking habits of Jos' residents are also legendary. It was a drinking town par excellence and most of its drinkers would put Loftus Versfeld on a Saturday afternoon to shame. And I'm only talking about the women.

More importantly, because of Jos' cosmopolitan nature and the large presence of missionaries from all religions, especially Christians and Muslims, conflict regularly broke out between religious groups. Two weeks before I landed in Jos[10] for the *Gulder Ultimate Search 4* the town was nearly reduced to ruins and close to 1 000 people died in the violence. When I arrived there was no sign of it.

The local supermarket stocked 49 different versions of the Bible. To many Nigerians, who in general believed God was white, the rejection of their old ideas and the acceptance of Christianity was a way of showing they were educated. It was linked to westernisation, which in turn implied that you were slightly better than the non-Christian backward people.

If you want to take the argument further, you could say that these black Christians really wanted to be white and strove to be white through their religion. I wouldn't go as far as that, but evangelists like the (white) German Reinhard Bonnke, who was a superstar in Nigeria, personified it. His extraordinary popularity among Nigerians definitely had something to do with the colour of his skin. He was one of many who, like the missionaries of old, entered the country in droves, but in his case not only to win souls, but also to take their money.

In Jos we stayed in oval shaped rondavels. The kitchen swarmed with cockroaches and our chef didn't speak English – at least not a version of English I could understand. The brown and marble linoleum floor was slightly uneven, but not uneven enough to trip over it. The creamy yellow curtains with their subtle though anatomically correct rose pattern (or could it have been tulips?) complimented

---

10 The previous year I exchanged the Nigerian circus for the set of Afrikaans *Idols*.

the colour of the walls (creamy yellow). Unfortunately the green, brown and blue stripes on the sheets and pillows clashed badly with the pink, red and brown psychedelic patterns on the blankets. I couldn't wait to meet the interior designer – I was convinced he would be a remarkable fellow. And once again – there weren't any bath plugs.

I went searching for pretty material in the local market, but I decided to spoil myself instead with a Rolex. At R50 it was a real bargain and it had the Nigerian authentication: the watch took 62 minutes to complete an hour. Days later I would wish that I could make time stand still, because I experienced something that I desperately wanted to rewrite and reshoot.

On Thursdays the market opened later so that the area could be cleaned. This meant that everyone took their rubbish and threw it on top of the previous week's rubbish, which in turn went on top of the previous week's rubbish. And there it stayed, until someone one day decided to put a match to the whole stinking lot. Every last Saturday of the month was sanitation day. No one was allowed on the streets, the roads were closed and large lorries drove around and sprayed everything with insecticide or disinfectant. I didn't want to know what they all were.

I also visited the museum (sorry I fibbed in the foreword). The museum was full of broken, dust-covered clay pots. Many of the exhibition pieces were stolen and the pieces of paper stuck to the wall that described the pieces were yellow with age, dog-eared and full of spelling errors.

In the library (yeah!) I tracked down a book about Jos' history as part of my research for the programme. The book was published in 1967 and written by one Leonard Plotnicov. One of the previous librarians had corrected all the factual errors in the book with a pen. While I paged through the book, the current librarian breathed over my shoulder as if the book was the library's sole prized possession.

The photocopying machine was out of order and when my phone rang, he kicked me out.

By this time we had worked out a basic formula for filming the *GUS*. We would find some or other deserted structure close to a place that could serve as a set and then we'd take lock, stock and barrel to the location. This accomplished, trees and bushes were chopped down to make a clear road, and power cables as well as water pipes were laid. We even had geysers. The generators worked 24 hours a day and satellites ensured we had internet and DStv.

On paper it seemed that we were in total control, but in reality this wasn't always the case. As happens so very often in Nigeria, the infrastructure is there, but not everything necessarily works all the time. As before, we were kilometres from the nearest sign of civilisation and Lagos was more than six hours away. The client was still on the everlasting lookout for mistakes in the programme, but renewed the contract each year.

The increasing popularity of the programme meant that more and more people wanted to take part in it and thousands arrived for the elimination rounds, which were held in those states that had the infrastructure to host them. States in the Muslim North, where alcohol was prohibited, wasn't part of the picture. The contestants were asked about their general health and as so many Nigerians couldn't swim it became a minimum requirement for participation.

This particular year we had to feed 220 people every day. This meant that the chefs had to slaughter every day. Slaughter like on the farm, because there weren't any supermarkets and butchers who could neatly cut up the carcass and pack it into portions in airtight bags or styrofoam. The Nigerian slaughtering process worked differently to what I remembered. First the bovine's legs were tied with a rope and then it could take several hours before the poor animal was slaughtered. It would lie there until someone cut his throat with a sharp knife. So on your way to the set, you walked past that night's dinner.

After the bovine bled to death, its hair had to be stripped off. This was usually done with a knife or a panga, but lazy butchers often threw some lamp oil over the animal and set it alight. It looked like a surreal burnt offering spectacle when the flames surrounded the animal. After all the hair was removed the skin and inner layer of fat was cut off. It was regarded as a delicacy and people usually fought to get it. They called it *pomo* and in the markets some stalls specialised in this delicacy.

The rest of the animal was cut up without the aid of a butcher's card. The intestines were not cleaned, but cooked. So it could easily happen that you got the last grass in the cow's large intestine with the piece of meat on your plate. The meat was always served well done and most of the time was as tough as the soles of a shoe. That could be why Nigerians always covered everything with pepper.

It was ironic that Nigerians had the same raw ingredients at their disposal as, for example, the Thai, but they used them so differently. Their meat was supplemented by a variety of starch dishes such as yam. One of the sauces they prepared with it looked exactly like snot. Yet every Nigerian will tell you about their wonderful food. I bet my late artist-friend Braam Kruger would have had some well-chosen remarks about the average Nigerian meal.

I'm sure it's not politically correct to criticise other cultures' eating customs. In each country I visit I try to eat some of the local food. In Nigeria I could only do it once and then I decided to insist on a chef who could prepare Western food.

There was also a popular fish dish called "point and kill". Barbels are regarded as a treat in Nigeria, but because of the weather it's better to keep them alive until just before they're cooked. In the neat restaurants in Lagos they swam around carefree in glass cases. You chose one and minutes later it was served. Point and kill. In the rural areas they swam around in plastic washing dishes until their fate was decided.

Snails were another special dish. I knew that the French also served snails and hid it behind the word *escargot*, but these snails were different. They were as large as a man's fist and were only found in certain places during certain parts of the year. People would spend the day in the jungle picking them up and then stand on the side of

the road to sell them. They were so popular there'd sometimes be queues to buy them.

Nigeria is a country where men wear dresses and hold hands when they walk, but homosexuality is against the law. The same mind-set might apply to their eating habits – they eat snails, but they don't touch sushi. They'll eat rats, but not pizza.

Adagldom Achaji Umary Gimba I, also known as the district head of Gwash, was the first traditional leader I met in Nigeria. Because Jos and the surrounding area were so rural, I was almost in daily contact with the locals. They fascinated me.

They were hardworking, but poor. They would greet you in a friendly manner, but they didn't want to talk. If you walked past them while they were eating, they would offer you bread, but they would demand money from you if you took a mealie from their crop.

At the local quarry men blasted the rocks with dynamite twice a day and used hammers to make the boulders smaller. Strong young men then broke the rocks into smaller pieces and the next group made them even smaller. The last lot, who made the gravel, were old women and children.

This was headman Gimba's chiefdom and he ruled it with an iron fist. His community also made money in other legal ways, such as renting out their land. In Nigeria every piece of land belongs to a tribe and even if you walk over it you have to pay. The money that chief Gimba was paid for the use of his jungle for the shoot upped his income substantially.

After a week or two's negotiations I eventually got an audience with him. I arrived at the agreed time, but had to wait for an hour before I could see his highness. His "palace", as it was referred to, was a mud hut with a corrugated iron roof that was slightly larger than those belonging to the rest of the community. Outside a pitch black BMW M5 graced his humble abode. It was a reasonably new model, but the signs were evident that the local government should seriously consider upgrading the roads. The only decent road in the area must have been tarred in the 1970s and could in all honesty no longer be called a tarred road.

The reception room of the house had two kinds of seating: large couches and plastic garden chairs. But most of his subordinates, even those dressed in suits for the occasion, preferred to sit at his feet and look up at the sage while he spoke his words of wisdom. It looked like those Children's Bible pictures of Jesus with all the children at his feet. Chief Gimba even had a halo: the only light streamed in through a small window behind his head.

He was a large, imposing man who carried himself like someone to whom people would show respect. He was almost blue black and wore a traditional garment. There were many people who faffed around him and they all had to remove their shoes before they could enter the room. He didn't speak English and his interpreter's English wasn't very good.

The purpose of my visit was to get information so that I could incorporate some local flavour in the form of stories, myths and anecdotes into the television series. Apparently there wasn't much to tell and the conversation progressed in a constipated manner. Chief Gimba was clearly amused by my discomfort.

**Chief Gimba**

When I arrived, I took my place on the chair next to his "throne". It was a Lazyboy with many hours on the clock. After a while I decided to sit on the floor like the rest of his subjects. Only then did he deign to tell me a story. He also insisted that I credit him with the story if I used it. According to him the story may only be told between August and October when the yam is harvested and so a sacrifice first had to be made at one of the many totems around the house to prevent the yam crop from damage because the story was being told at the wrong time. Of course I had to pay for the sacrifice.

Warning: If you read this story before August or after October, there is a chance that some of your garden plants will die.

"A man married two women (as was the custom). One's name was Akwe (she cooked), the other's name was Awoerka (she didn't cook). Both of them become pregnant at the same time and returned to their maternal homes to have their children. The man wanted a son and promised to slaughter a cow for the woman who bore him a son.

Akwe had a son and Awoerka a girl. While the two women were on their way back to their husband's house, they met each other near the river. While Akwe bathed, Awoerka grabbed her son and left her daughter behind. When Akwe arrived at the tribal village a feast was held for Awoerka because she brought home a son. She became the favourite wife, while Akwe became the servant who had to clean and cook.

When the son – his name was Tsala – grew up he was sent out to become a hunter. On his first hunt he fell from a horse (this part I found especially funny, because I have never seen a horse in Nigeria, but the chief stuck to his story) and broke his back. He lay in the veldt and there was no way to get a message home that he needed help. Eventually the animals who found him decided to send a bird to the house.

The father and Tsala's biological mother, Akwe, understood the message, but not Awoerka. After years of oppression Akwe eventually decided to stand up for her rights. She told Awoerka if she called the boy and he didn't get up it was proof that he wasn't Awoerka's child. Of course the boy didn't get up. But when Akwe called him his broken back miraculously healed and he ran straight back to his biological mother.

Everyone went back home and a huge feast was held. Awoerka's daughter refused to go back to her biological mother and the woman became an outcast in her own community."

This is a short, edited version of the story that was told in an extremely leisurely fashion over a period of two hours. The audience took another 30 minutes to make sure I clearly understood the story and its ethical implications. Then I had to eat yam – one simply cannot hear the story without eating yam. If not, it brought bad luck. Yam tasted yucky.

Had I known of the bad luck that would befall the production team and myself shortly afterwards, I might have eaten more of the yam.

Two days later I again contacted chief Gimba so that I could take a photograph of him. This time there was no sign of his loyal subjects. The jovial old man with his broad smile wasn't the same man who told me the story. When I started to take off my shoes he rejected my attempt with a gesture and talked to me in fluent English.

Mudiaga Anthony Ogadje was like any of the aspirant contestants: an ordinary guy from an ordinary home. He dreamt of winning the GUS competition to create a better life for himself. He had recently graduated in geography from the Delta State University, where he also was on the local swimming team.

His mother was an ordinary civil servant and his father was deceased; he was their only child. Mudiaga's favourite musician was Shaggy and he wanted to become a film star. Like most people in Nigeria he was unemployed. The *GUS 4* was his chance to realise all his dreams and ensure an easier life for his mother.

From the moment we started shooting the series Mudiaga attracted my attention. He was intelligent, well read and had a six-pack of epic proportions. Like Vaughn he knew what his strengths and weaknesses were and he played a role rather than showing his true personality. He was also hyperactive, almost never slept and irritated his fellow contestants with his over-the-top enthusiasm. Mudiaga's sole purpose in life was to win the competition and he was without a doubt the strongest contestant.

Because he was so restless, I suspected he was using steroids, but the medical tests revealed nothing. I was worried about him because he looked like he could have a blow out any second. I asked the doctor to do extra tests on him, but he said everything was in order.

The contestants' instruction for episode 6 was simple. They had to row over the lake in a canoe, then run up a hill and get their clue. Then they had to go back over the lake. The first person who arrived back at the starting point and who could solve the riddle was the winner. The activity was filmed by eight different cameras, of which most were placed on the far side of the lake, the side to which the contestants rowed.

Mudiaga was well ahead of the pack and raced up the hill minutes before the rest. When we looked at the recordings again, we saw how out of breath he was when he took the riddle and that he sat down with his hand over his heart. When the other contestants started running up the hill, he jumped up and ran back to his canoe. Instead of getting into the canoe Mudiaga, for some inexplicable reason, jumped straight into the lake. He disappeared below the water and never surfaced again. He didn't even flounder. He simply jumped in and sank like a stone.

I was on the Border and saw people die in front of me. Some of them were friends, but you expect people to die in a war. You don't expect it to happen during the filming of a reality television programme.

The other contestants stood around bewildered on the bank. The lifesavers jumped in and started searching for him, but couldn't find him. People walked up and down along the bank and prayed out loud. Most members of the production team couldn't swim, so there was a tangible feeling of helplessness while the few people who could swim searched for his body for 45 minutes.

When they eventually found his body, the medical team tried for nearly an hour to revive him, but to no avail. Mudiaga Anthony Ogadje's death was captured on a multi-camera shoot and nothing could save him. After the body was laid down on the stretcher, somebody took off his Gulder T-shirt in case someone at the hospital phoned the media. The *spin* had already started.

In the midst of the shock the reality of the situation kicked in pretty quickly. The director and I were the only two *oyibos* on the shoot and also the most senior people. A Nigerian just died while we were making a television programme and the local police would certainly have their own theory about the events. Against the advice of the other senior Nigerians in the team we immediately phoned the big bosses in Lagos. The other members of the team wanted to get their own story straight first. Everyone was afraid they might lose their jobs, or even worse, be accused of culpable homicide.

The other contestants were sent back to their camp. They were told that Mudiaga wasn't dead, but on his way to hospital. By the time we got back to the base, the internet connection was cut and our cell phones were confiscated. Our own security people cordoned off the base to prevent anyone from entering or leaving. They were in turn surrounded by local police who prevented anyone from going anywhere.

There was a feeling of total devastation. People sat around and gazed into vacant space. Prayer groups spontaneously formed among the contestants and production team. Whether they prayed for Mudiaga's peace or their own safety I couldn't say.

In Nigeria the guy with the most effective security and best contacts is the one who wins a stand-off. Our Lagos contacts had more influence than the local police chief and by the next morning, when the big shots arrived from Lagos, the local police cordon was withdrawn and we could move around freely again. Not that we had anything to do. Production was temporarily put on hold, we had no internet access and our cell phones were still confiscated

Then a strange thing happened. All the original tapes that recorded Mudiaga's drowning disappeared after an edited version was quickly made to prove Nigerian Breweries' innocence. The one thing that could have caused problems was the safety officer's decision to keep all the lifesavers on the side of the lake where the race started. To save money there was no motor-powered rescue boat. The lifesavers had to swim about 100 metres across the lake to start searching for Mudiaga.

According to the post-mortem reports Mudiaga drowned, but I still believe that he had a heart attack. That possibility was never investigated.

Then negotiations with his family began. The big shots from Lagos arrived with beer in hand to talk to the family about the money they had to pay as damages for their loss. An amount was agreed on, the single mother buried her only son and the series, although it was shortened, continued.

Each programme ended with Mudiaga's photograph, but we were soon instructed to shorten the airtime dedicated to him with each programme. By the last episode there was no reference to him. He was written out of the series and out of the history.

Of course, such an incident could cause a great deal of damage to a trademark, but the cold, calculated way the matter was handled left me dumbfounded.

I often think of Mudiaga and whether we could have done anything to save his life. I wonder where he would have been today had he won and how different his family's (and his own) life would have been.

What I do know is that the programme's viewership suddenly rocketed after the incident. *Na wa*[11] …

---

11 A Nigerian expression when you know you can't change anything about a situation. "Na wa" is Yoruba for *c'est la vie*.

# DIARY OF THE END OF A MARRIAGE
## Enugu, 2008

I HAD AN OVERWHELMING feeling of déjà-vu when I landed at the Murtalla Mohammed airport for the fourth time. The Nigerians' smugness still knew no bounds and I was welcomed with a story of an American who acted the big man but met his match in a major way.

This time it was the rapper Akon's turn. Akon, originally from Senegal, was no stranger to controversy.[12] He was a man who walked around with the bravado of the big rappers.

Akon liked to do the crowd surf thing during his shows. He would dive in among the audience who would literally carry him on their hands. But as 50 Cent had found out the hard way, things were done slightly differently in Lagos. Before Akon tried his party trick in Lagos he was warned that the crowd was full of area boys who didn't like him very much. To his detriment he decided to ignore the good advice and went crowd surfing.

When he reappeared on stage he was only in his underpants. The

---

12 The year before Akon was in trouble in Honduras after he simulated sex with a 14-year-old girl during a stage show. Two months later he was in trouble again when he hit a 15-year-old fan at one of his shows. For this transgression he had to do community service and pay an admission of guilt fine of $250.

rest of his outfit, including his watch, jewellery, trousers and even his socks and Timberland boots were removed from his body while he was in the crowd.

Here we go again – welcome to Lagos. By 2008 some things had certainly improved, but other habits die hard. One very annoying habit was our client's constant interference during the production of the *Gulder Ultimate Search* (*GUS*). It became routine for Nigerian Breweries to fire at least one person by the end of each series. So even before the series started in earnest everyone was already in a state of panic. This year the dubious honour would go to a woman (one of those who used tears to get her way when the director and I didn't listen to her).

By this time it was estimated that a third of the country regularly watched the programme. Beer sales kept on growing and Nigerian Breweries tightened its grip on the series even further. In the past it was my and the director's privilege to choose most of the participants. In this way we could ensure that there were enough interesting people in the mix to ensure some action and exciting viewing. But this time round the client ignored all our suggestions and chose all ten participants themselves – one more boring than the other.

By the time I arrived in Nigeria the number of entries were already reduced from about 50 000 to 12 000. This smaller group then took part in regional trials countrywide. Not that there was a trial in every corner of the country – there were parts of Nigeria where no self-respecting Nigerian would be seen dead. The local stadium was used for the trials. If you visit the different stadiums in Nigeria you can easily see which governor stole the most money and which of them put in some effort to retain a modicum of respect.

The largest comedy show in Nigeria was the tapes of the regional trials where hopeful candidates tried to talk their way into the competition, even if they didn't have a chance in hell of being chosen.

The tapes where they showed off their swimming skills were even funnier. Apart from the Nigerians' smugness of which I was now painfully aware, I also got to see their determination.

The process was simple. Everyone stood in a line next to the swimming pool and was asked one by one on camera: "Can you swim?" Without exception the answer was always "yes". Few of them could swim, but some tried their best to hide it. A trick that was regularly employed was to walk on the bottom of the pool and wave their arms about. Others looked like extraordinary top loader washing machines as they hit the water as much as possible in the hope that they would float. After yet another potential participant had to be rescued, her excuse was: "But I *can* swim. The water was just too deep."

For the first two programmes of the series we used the material from the trials with comical music and humorous comments. Compared to these non-starters our future heroes, the last ten, looked like demi gods.

After the regional trials 40 participants were chosen who would go to Sea School. Sea School was in Lagos, but there was also a Mountain School, Desert School and various other schools across

the country. Young Nigerians did community service at these schools for a year according to the National Youth Service Corps system. For that year they were employed by the state, lived in barracks, were taught basic discipline and worked in areas where they didn't have any family or friends. It was supposed to help the 153 ethnic groups in the country to get to know each other better. In any event that was the theory behind it.

With the *GUS* we also tried to be as ethnically diverse as possible, but not because of politically correct reasons. Participants from various ethnic groups were the easiest way to attract a large number of viewers from all groups. The Sea School group was reduced to eighteen before the final ten were announced at a gala event.

The night was just as stylish as an official function of Tshwane's mayor. The VIPs were allocated special seats, with better food and drink than the other tables. People fought to get tickets for the evening and the Hummers and other expensive vehicles packed the parking area. People wore their most glamorous outfits and in general tried to look as important as possible. There were speeches and more speeches.

In short, it was the kind of event that drives me to drink. Nigeria has a very interesting sales system for liquor. When you order a whisky or cognac by the tot you pay between R20 and R40. But if you order a bottle it costs you only 10% more than in a liquor store. It therefore made much more economic sense to buy a bottle. This also meant that you drank much more than you had to or intended to. Alcohol is a nasty little devil that exposes certain parts of your personality that you don't really want people to know about. After a few weeks of the frustration so peculiar to Lagos it also unleashes aggressive behaviour. You can keep the pose until you take that final drink that tips the scales and then all hell breaks loose. And in Lagos this is never a good idea, as it takes a small thing to let loose the thinly veiled aggression, and besides, there are far too many people in black uniforms carrying AK47s. So, it's far better to smile and solve problems in a reasonable manner.

Unfortunately, that night I found out that the bottle of Johnny Walker that I helped polish off would not put me in a frame of mind where problem solving was my forte.

Our producers eventually found a hotel that was almost on standard (although it didn't have any bath plugs). They made a mean dagwood, it was reasonably clean and the bar didn't allow the kind of ladies who won't leave men alone. The bar was usually crowded with European pilots who hit the bottle as hard as we did.

Hotel Devine (I still don't know whether it's a spelling error or if the name has a deeper meaning) was situated in a compound in one of Lagos' better areas. This meant that you had to go through security gates to get to the hotel, which were manned by – you guessed it – men with AK47s. They were ordinary policemen but the area was actually controlled by the area boys, who didn't even have weapons.

The guard at the security gate was a pipsqueak who didn't know what to do with all his power, even though he was armed. He might not have been Nigerian. After a night of irritation, two weeks of frustration and way too much Johnny Walker Black we were met by a long queue of cars in front of the security gate. Everyone hooted and some drivers switched off their vehicles. Our driver didn't have an answer when I asked him what was wrong.

Then I made a serious error of judgement by getting out of the car and walking to the gate. In Lagos everyone felt big and strong behind the steering wheels, but when you got out you exposed yourself to elements you didn't want to experience first-hand. People shouted at each other furiously. I couldn't understand what was going on … until I saw the two area boys. They were easily recognisable by their cocky attitude. The two scoundrels had closed the gate and were refusing to let people enter unless they paid an "entry fee".

This was a well-off neighbourhood and the people in the cars were probably residents or visitors to the neighbourhood. I couldn't understand why they were waiting so patiently for something to happen. Actually I was furious that they docilely allowed the two gangsters to screw with them.

Fortified by Johnny's courage and an excess of adrenaline as a result of pure irritation I walked to the gate and, without giving it a second thought, opened it. The two area boys were so gobsmacked that they didn't immediately click what was happening, because the cars started to drive through without delay. However, as it sunk in they started to move in my direction. Even the guy with the AK47 disappeared into the background. Although all the motorists benefited from my action nobody stopped to help. This was clearly my problem.

I decided that the car would be the safest place, but the area boys reached me before I could get to it. They were beside themselves with rage and started shouting at me, clearly not used to being treated like this. I got flashbacks of Kayode and knew that if I showed fear it would be all over for me.

I employed my usual tactics by trying to smooth things over, but nobody listened to me. They all shouted at the top of their voices. Funnily enough the guy with the AK47 came closer and tried to protect me. When he pushed the barrel of his gun into one area boy's face, it was pushed away with contempt.

They were humiliated in front of the very people whom they were supposed to intimidate and it wasn't going down well at all. Suddenly I was surrounded by a mass of people. Some attacked me, others defended me. The area boys had now started to realise that they wouldn't necessarily win this fight and also saw how the sources of bribes were now passing by.

My director, brave man that he was, put it so eloquently: "I think it's time to fuck off." Truer words were never spoken and in the confusion we quickly went back to our car. When I got into the car one area boy shouted: "I live in your country, I don't tell you what to do; don't tell me what to do in mine." I realised he thought I was a Brit. "Hey, arsehole!" I shouted through the window of our moving car, "I'm not from London, I'm from Jo'burg. So fuck you."

He didn't see that one coming. I didn't even look back to see how his shock registered. I immediately went back to the bar for some more Johnny to help calm me down.

This year our destination was Enugu. It was the capital of the state Enugu, better known as "Biafra", where most residents were Igbos. Biafra should never have been part of Nigeria, and it can only be attributed to the colonial authority's idiosyncratic sense of geography. This very geography meant that the historical Kingdom of Benin is today part of Nigeria and not of Benin.

The Biafran, as the older reader or history nerds will recall, already launched a war of independence, but lost. In 1966 an Igbo general took over power in Nigeria with a coup d'état. The Yorubas and Hausas didn't like that one bit and performed their own coup d'état. Hundreds of Igbos were murdered in the process and they decided to secede from Nigeria. At that time they already knew they had the largest part of the oil resources under their control. On 6 July 1967 the Nigerian army invaded Biafra and the civil war that lasted for 18 months caused widespread famine.

The central government stopped the supply of all food stock to the area and won the war in the end by letting people die of hunger. Much the same technique that the British used against the Boers in the war of 1899-1902. The government didn't shy away from attacking civilians and their MiG17's regularly bombarded Red Cross hospitals.

Even though they lost the war, the independence ideal still burns strongly in the hearts of many Igbos who feel they are being exploited by central government. The Biafran war was largely about the right to self-determination, but control of the oil fields also played a central role. The Movement for the Emancipation of the Niger

Delta (MEND), which received such a great deal of media attention over the past few years is, in a way, a continuation of this struggle. However, they are more concerned about oil rights and power than about pursuing a freedom ideal. This does not mean that the Biafran liberation movement is no longer active. There were various underground terrorist groups, but also legal political parties who were struggling to get into mainstream national politics.

It is prohibited to display the Biafran flag. When you drive along the main road through Enugu in the mornings, it's quite an amusing sight to see the police cadets clambering up against palm trees to remove the Biafran flags that were hung out during the night. They wave defiantly from the main road.

Enugu is not a town for sissies. Here I openly encountered opposition against me as outsider. People from the outside weren't welcome and weren't trusted. Even the production team, who consisted mainly of Yorubas tread lightly. The first time I could visit the city on my own, I was asked to leave the market. My armed guard was too scared to walk into the market with me.

People aren't kidnapped in Lagos because of the traffic jams. You wouldn't be able to get your victim away from the scene quickly enough. Enugu was another story. Port Harcourt and Enugu made it to the top two on the list for the most kidnappings. Jetta, our head of security, took his job very seriously and there were almost more guards than production members. When he called me his "million dollar man" I thought he'd taken a liking to me. Later I realised that he was referring to the ransom that kidnappers would ask for me.

The moment we arrived, I knew it wasn't going to be an easy year. Our accommodation was in a road building camp outside of Enugu, which was last used in the seventies. It was in an area where a maize seed grew to an edible mealie within six weeks. You can just imagine how densely wooded it was. Small huts were scattered all around but there was no central gathering place. It posed big challenges to

Our digs in Enugu

a production like ours where decisions had to be taken from minute
to minute. The heat was oppressive even though it was the cooler
season and people were blown off their feet in the tropical storms.

Someone had tried their damndest to make our huts liveable, but
with little success. Thirty years worth of grime sat against the walls
and the electrical wiring was open. The hollow wooden walls crawled
with rats that tried to gnaw their way to the food they could smell
inside. Every night, from sunset to sunrise, for four endless weeks. It
was like Chinese water torture. And you couldn't do anything about it.

The mattresses were so cheap that the dent of your body remained
behind after you got up. I solved this problem by sleeping next to
my previous night's imprint until I reached the end of the mattress.
Then for the following three nights I slept across, once again next
to the previous night's imprint.

For some reason all the electric plugs were up against the roof.
The one above my bed worried me – I was afraid it might fall down
during the night. The toilet in our bathroom was kept upright by an
unsteady wooden scaffolding. The plumber, who certainly couldn't
have passed his final exam, had the amazing brainwave to join the

warm and cold water pipes in the shower. The weather was so humid that our Niara notes started to get musty.

It was difficult to understand why someone would fight for such a place. But at the stroke of five every morning the cleaners flocked into our little kingdom to wash, dust or polish something. A rude note on the door put a quick stop to this early morning invasion. After that nobody entered unless they were invited.

Our scanty accommodation was only the start of our problems. A twenty minute drive along a remote potholed mountain road took us from our huts to the set and nobody was allowed to go to the set without police escort. It was difficult to move around and get your work done.

This particular year Nigerian Breweries decided at an early stage who had to win – a tall, limp fellow named Michael. He had already mastered the art of falling over his feet, he now only had to try and win one of the challenges. The final day's shoot, which would determine the winner, was even postponed so that he could be healthy and strong enough to win.

I'm not the greatest fan of authority and I know that I can be a little irresponsible at times, but the working conditions forced me to do something that rubbed everyone up the wrong way. If one's movements are limited to the set every day, the inside of a vehicle, the edit suite and your filthy digs, cabin fever is bound to set in pretty quickly. Irrespective of how or where you look for distraction that feeling will only disappear when you do something reckless.

I was very curious to see what the village outside the gates of our camp looked like. I'd been smoking a fat spliff and found my way there without being noticed by our watchful armed men. In the village I quickly found a drinking spot, consisting of a corrugated roof with four stumps for pillars. They had cold beer and played James Brown's "Living in America" over and over. A cool breeze lifted my bruised spirit. How refreshing!

Scarcely half a beer later my peace was seriously disturbed by wailing sirens and policemen who descended on the bar. Jetta, sunglasses and all, got out of the front twin cab. The rest of the clients took to their heels, and I was courteously requested to get into the vehicle and taken back to the camp. I wasn't even allowed to finish my beer. The owner, a cranky old woman whose tits went so far south that they wobbled about like wet tea bags beneath her T-shirt shouted I believe obscene things in Igbo at me. How did I lose my charm? How could this affable oni ochi (the Igbo word for "white man") not be her favourite person?

When I tried to revisit the same bar a week later, she chased me away with a stick before I could sit down properly.

My bitching and moaning about Enugu will stop right here. If you win a holiday to Enugu, give it to your greatest enemy. And if you are offered a job there, make sure that you are paid enough to make it worth while.

Two days before I left Enugu, there was an attack on the governor of the state. It happened two minutes from where we stayed and six people died. On the way to the airport we passed the vehicle. It was no longer recognisable as a Mercedes Benz and had more holes than a tea-strainer. I had no idea how he survived the attack.

Back in Lagos we had to attend the party where the winner was introduced to the public.

EXTERIOR: A street in Lagos
It's late afternoon and the camera is in the middle of the street. On both sides of the road there are three to four rows of people who strain forward.

CLOSE UP
You can see the excitement on the people's faces. They are dirt poor and wear torn T-shirts with washed out African patterns, but they anticipate something truly inspiring.

EXTERIOR: The club
People congregate outside the building and there are Gulder flags everywhere. A red carpet leads into the building. The people are dressed well. They don't look like rich people, but one can see that they earn a salary.

INTERIOR: The club
The interior of the club is draped in red, back and gold material – Gulder's official colours. The venue is packed with prosperous guests. The most important people sit right at the front, closest to the stage. The red carpet goes from the outside of the club to the stage. Slowly you become aware of screaming sirens.

EXTERIOR: The street

In the distance you can see black police vehicles that are escorting someone. The windows are tinted and the sirens are becoming louder. The people next to the road push slightly forward, but not far enough to be hit by the vehicles. When the first police vehicle moves past the camera, you become aware of something strange. A man far taller than two metres is sitting on a small 50 cc quad. His legs are so long that his knees nearly touch his ears. He is wearing a Roman helmet that almost hangs over his eyes. The people next to the road cheer him on. The camera starts to shake as the camera man goes into a fit of laughter. Nobody else thinks it's funny.

EXTERIOR: The club

There is a commotion among the crowd when they realise their hero is on his way. They make room for the police vehicle and then close the road to be closer to their hero who at this point is struggling to see where he is going. He hits the bottom step and nearly falls off his quad. The crowd cheer harder.

CLOSE UP

You can see how the hero struggles to disengage himself from the quad. The helmet is almost on his nose by now. He trips over the first step while he tries to lift up the helmet. Someone pushes the quad out of the way.

INTERIOR: The club

The people, except the most important ones right at the front, jump up and cheer. He smiles broadly, the helmet in his hand by now. He waves at the crowd while he walks along the red carpet.

FADE TO BLACK

Beam me up, Scotty. It's time to go home.

# I ♥ NIGERIA

Ada, 2009

Yeah, I am a sucker for punishment. It's six years after my first visit to Nigeria and here I am again in the middle of nowhere thanks to the *Gulder Ultimate Search* (*GUS*). Three presenters, two directors and an endless number of humid venues later. I'm the sole South African survivor from the original team.

I was here for every series with the exception of number 3 (2006), when I had to choose between two months in a Nigerian jungle or to host my own talk show, *SaterdagNag*, on kykNet and be a judge for the Afrikaans *Idols*. It was a relatively easy choice. For the first time I could earn more money in South Africa than in Nigeria and I had my own dressing room with French champagne and caviar. I realised that it was far less hassle to be in front of the camera than behind it. I didn't like it, but I only found that out after a while. More about that in my next book, *My Year of Being Famous*[13].

Meanwhile I started a weird love affair with Nigeria. I realised that everyone who raves against the country was in fact referring to Lagos, but Lagos isn't Nigeria. With each of my visits to places like Calabar, Obudu, Enugu, Jos and now to Ada in the state of Osun this West African onion was peeled away further.

I discovered that Nigeria becomes even more absurd the closer

---

13 It did take me ten years to write *Witboy in Africa,* so don't hold your breath. *My Year of Being Famous* might be on your Christmas list for 2020.

you get to its core. If you have a keen sense of observation, you'll notice that many people have a so-called Western, but also a village, personality. The Nigerians are proud of their traditional customs, even though they know outsiders find them strange. They pride themselves on their weirdness.

What makes the country so fascinating is that it has a functional economy, but does not adhere to the generally accepted rules of the business world. If you want to do business in Nigeria, you'll find that they work according to rules that would be considered absurd in many other countries or simply illegal. As Nigeria is the sixth largest oil producer in the world, it gets away with many weird business practices.

About 153 million people who speak more than two hundred languages live there, but the three largest ethnic groups don't like each other much. According to Nigerian generalisation the Yorubas are the artistic types, the Igbos the business people and the Hausas the committed Muslims. The Igbos, who already lost in the Biafran war, are the group who are most excluded from public life and this is why most of them end up as drug dealers in South Africa and other countries. In a conversation in a bar in Ada, *GUS'* new presenter, Bob Manuel Udokwu, leaned over to me after a couple of beers and whispered conspiratorially in my ear that they were trying to get rid of him because he was an Igbo. The rest of the team were Yorubas.

Meanwhile I picked up the habit of saying *abi?* at the end of my sentences, which is the Nigerian equivalent of the Afrikaans "nè!" and I knew when to pull up my shoulders and say *na wa!* I also learnt that if you drove down Awolowo Street in Lagos on a Friday afternoon, you'll encounter a police road block every 100 metres and you will be expected to pay for each of the already drunk policemen's next beer.

> *"Police turn extortionists at Ago Palace Way"*
> "The activities of units of the Nigerian police in Okota is becoming very worrisome. Everyday at 7 p.m. they set two or three checkpoints along the ever busy Ago Palace Way. According to residents of the area on an ordinary day the traffic gridlock is bad enough cause by workers driving hom from work. One can imagine the utter chaos resulting from the Police checkpoint. It would be a good work if the Police men are there to confront armed robbers or any other terror gangs menacing Lagosians. But they are simply there to extort money from private car owners and commercial buses drivers. Residents are hereby appealing to the Lagos State government to check the unwholesome activities of these police especially now that the country is rebranding."
>
> *- Daily Independent*, 30 June 2009

And "rebrand" was exactly what Nigeria started to do. Since my first visit to the country there were large-scale changes and development. Under pressure from the International Monetary Fund and the World Bank, Nigeria tightened its banking legislation. Bank owners were no longer protected by their mates in government. They had to put down deposits to prevent sudden bankruptcies, which in the past were used as an excuse to steal people's money.

For the first time ordinary citizens had access to credit. In the past all transactions were in cash, whether you wanted to buy a house, a car or a new pair of shoes. By making credit available a middle class was created who could own their own homes and afford new cars.

Where Lagos previously had the musty colour of the tropics, a large number of buildings boasted new coats of paint. It had a lot to do with the large-scale influx of South African money. Shopping centres sprang up like mushrooms and sold real Mont Blanc and Patek Philippe. Branches of Exclusive Books, Game and Shoprite opened up. At the local Nando's a quarter chicken and chips costs an upmarket R65 and is regarded as a posh night out.

The Mega Plaza, which was owned by Lebanese and in 2004 was still the only shopping centre (term used loosely) in Lagos, burnt down under mysterious circumstances after the South Africans started building their own shopping centres. Fortunately for the owners of the Mega Plaza they insured the building three weeks before it was burnt to the ground. South African money and influence weren't always received with open arms by Nigerians, but they regarded it as a necessary evil. Since 1994 South Africa overtook Nigeria as the leader of Africa and the average Nigerian didn't take it that well.

The Lagos that I encountered in 2009 was vastly different from the one I got to know in 2004. At the airport the immigration officers' pulpit was lower and the queue where you had to get in line right at the back had disappeared. Not that the officials were friendlier, but at least you no longer required the services of Captain to move safely through passport control. The city even had some residential areas that had tarred roads without potholes, security gates and peace and quiet like the residents of Dainfern can only dream about.

The films shown on the local television channels also no longer had the logo in the corner indicating that it was illegally copied and broadcast without the necessary rights. And all the Heinz Winckler videos, which were repeatedly shown on television six years ago, were something of the past.

For the average Lagosian few things changed. The fact that there are fewer beggars on the streets is not an indication that people no longer have to beg for a living. It's because Lagos' new governor, Babatunde Fashola, simply sent out a few trucks to collect everyone and return them to the villages they came from. The cattle and goat enclosures below the highway off-ramp were cleared away and truck repairs were no longer conducted from the sidewalks. Lagos started a cleaning process, even though it was only superficial.

Some things remain the same, like the ritual of handing over money. When you pay someone money with your left hand they will put it on the ground before they pick it up with their right hand. According to Nigerians your right hand is the hand of peace and your left hand is the hand of misfortune. If you put money that comes from a left hand into your pocket, things will not go well for you in the future.

Despite the "rebranding" law enforcement hasn't improved one iota. The police still abuse their power and terrorise the local residents to enrich themselves, rather than maintain law and order. In a country where the minimum wage is R350 per month and the average journalist hardly earns three times that amount, even the guardians of freedom of speech write for kickbacks. Nobody pays for crime stories – therefore they seldom appear in the newspaper.

Strangely, most Lagosians are mortally afraid of the crime in Johannesburg. The only news they get from South Africa are the inserts in *Carte Blanche*. Their entire perception of South Africa is therefore based on what appears on *Carte Blanche*.

Safety tips for Lagos according to a local newspaper:

1. Avoid stray bullets by lying down flat or taking cover during shootout between police and armed robbers. Avoid watching, it is no rehearsal or film show.

2. Engrave or print your vehicle registration number on your car's windscreen and accessories.

3. Do not keep your engine running while discussing with guest.
4. Remove any object which can aid an intruder in your house e.g. ladder, hammer, axe etc.
5. Avoid sudden and unfriendly offers of soft drink, beer, fruits or food from people unknown to you.
6. Don't board a taxi with strangers.
7. Never leave checking your windows, doors and security lights before you go to sleep to the servants.
8. Help raise alarm any time a neighbour is in distress.

*This Day*, July 2009

The governor of the state of Osun played golf every afternoon of the week. How did I know that? For the sixth *GUS* the entire team stayed at the MicCom Golf Hotel and Resort in Ada.

After all the discomfort and suffering we had to endure during the previous year with regard to accommodation we at last had a taste of the good life. In the lobby of the MicCom Golf Hotel was a colour photocopy of a certificate that stated that the hotel was one of the best hundred hotels in Nigeria in 2004. And there was a photograph of the former president Olusegun Obasanjo when he officially opened the hotel.

I didn't know what the other 99 hotels looked like, but this one did have a bath plug. Only one. I asked for it first. So it was my property. When other people wanted to bath, they borrowed mine. I had a nice arrangement going; I exchanged it for dagga, biscuits, honey to put in my rooibos tea and cognac.

At night around ten I cooled off in the hotel's swimming pool by smoking a joint and drinking cognac after the day's hard work.

In my opinion the hotel's chef is the best cook in all of Nigeria. He prepared the most delicious prawns, steak and smoked chicken. He also had a special touch with roasted, flying squirrel, which he imaginatively served with chips and a carrot and cucumber salad. He did not remove the head, paws or tail. The quirky squirrel that I was served sat neatly on the plate and wore a look of total astonishment. Like the true adventurer that I am I did not flinch once and I gnawed the squirrel flesh off the bones with relish.

He bought the squirrels from one of the hunters in the area. The hunters' guns were made by a local ironsmith and were simple contraptions that consisted of a piece of wood and a metal barrel. A bent pin was the hammer that made the shot go off, but the barrel was made in such a way that the cartridge case stayed behind. The trigger was a bent nail that was fastened to the barrel by a spring. The ironsmith was willing to sell me this ingenious invention for R35, but I wasn't sure how it would be received at customs control at OR Tambo so I declined the offer. When we shot in the jungle outside of Ada, we heard the hunters' shots all day and we feverishly prayed that they knew where we were. In the afternoon when we drove back to the hotel, they stood next to the road with the spoils of the hunt.

Some of the residents of the state of Osun believed that some people were reincarnated as goats. The goats were all over the show and roamed free, and people patiently drove around them, but this did not mean that on occasion they were not served up for dinner. I suspect there were guidelines as to which goats could be slaughtered and which not, but I never found out what they were.

Tony, the guy who makes sure that someone from Nigerian Breweries is fired each year, welcomed me to Ada with these prophetic words: "Hallo, Deon. Love is not sustainable on its own."

Everyone was scared of Tony and his words to me would become true in a way I could never foresee.

The latest edition of the *GUS* was one of the most popular. For the first time the production team was acknowledged and even the firing psychopath Tony had no problem with the production. He would have dearly loved to change the music, because it was written by someone he didn't like but we didn't let him get away with it. We all have to make small sacrifices to keep the world turning.

The new director Johan, a sterling fellow, didn't take any nonsense and soon everyone knew exactly what was expected of them. By this time the *GUS* production was like a well-oiled machine. Everyone knew what they had to do; we sorted out the logistical problems and surprises were few and far between. This time round everything was so much easier that I even had time to play around with ideas for new Nigerian reality programmes.

### Fear Factor Nigeria

As Nigerians already eat the stuff that nauseate other people such as snails, snakes and cockroaches, but don't understand the concept of sushi (somebody nearly vomited on me when I told them about it), I suggested that they be forced to eat it in *Fear Factor Nigeria*. By the way, many of them are disgusted by pizza. And where other people have to crawl over a precipice on cables, Nigerians could simply be asked to swim a few metres.

### The Apprentice Nigeria

Here we are looking for someone who can embezzle the most money in the most creative way possible. We can use members of párliament as participants, and definitely the governor who was caught red-handed with 200 million dollars in cash in his house.

### Big Brother Nigeria

When you put a lot of Nigerians in one house, the chances are good that one of them will be a member of the 419 syndicate. 419 is the Nigerian penalty code for fraud. The syndicates wait until you go on holiday before they gain access to your house and sell it. When you return someone else is living in your house and has (falsified) papers to prove his ownership. The winner will be the sham agent who gets away with the money without being prosecuted. To pull that off he'll have to give half the money to someone in the prosecutor's office or his father will have to be well connected to prevent prosecution.

While everything in Nigeria went swimmingly, things at home started going horribly wrong. My visits to Nigeria always put pressure on my and Pauli's relationship and initially I thought we were just going through a bad patch.

But Pauli, the one whom I had hoped would be by my side until my dying breath, developed a roving eye. One thing led to the other and a week before the end of the series I was officially informed by SMS that my marriage of sixteen years was on the rocks. It felt as if I was on the Border and got a Dear Johnny. I was totally blindsided. It's difficult to describe your emotions when you are floored by something you don't see coming.

I soon learnt that powerlessness is a stronger emotion than jealousy. Like Tony said: "Love on its own is not sustainable." It was all so absurd that I wondered whether Tony wasn't in cahoots with a medicine man that bewitched people and had had a "spell" put on me to get back at me for all the times I'd disagreed with him. PAULI, Pauli … pauli.

Through it all the show had to go on. My Nigerian family was my strong support system while I was actually falling apart.

I was forced to concentrate on what I was there to do and I was much more focused. My analyses of the participants were sharper, my writing more polished and even the fact that my cell phone was stolen from my room couldn't faze me.

Back in Lagos I had my own ultimate experience.

The Shrine in Lagos is a legendary night club that opened its doors for the first time in the seventies. It started as a refuge for people who didn't agree with the government, a little like Jameson's in Commissioner Street in Johannesburg during the apartheid years. Jameson's spiritual leader was James Phillips, and Fela Kuti fulfilled the same role at The Shrine. Kuti was a legendary musician who broke every music rule but still reached the top. He died of HIV/Aids in 1997.

He criticised the government of the day in his lyrics and irritated the hell out of them. He was eventually sent to jail because he allegedly transgressed some foreign currency laws, but after his imprisonment he was even more focused. It was during the time when World Music went big and Kuti proclaimed his government's misdoings to the outside world with songs that were up to 27 minutes in length. Kuti wasn't the military leaders' blue-eyed boy. To show him who was boss, soldiers attacked The Shrine and cold-bloodedly killed many people in the club. Kuti's mother, an academic and the first woman in Nigeria to get her drivers licence, was thrown out of a window. She later died due to complications caused by the fall.

The Shrine has always stood for freedom of thought and individuality. After Kuti's death it fell into disrepair, but in 2000 it was revived by his son, Femi, also a prominent musician. It had always been my dream to visit The Shrine, but because I usually spent so little time in Lagos, I never had the chance. For someone like me a visit to The Shrine was like a visit to Mecca. It was one of those things you had to do to die a peaceful death.

For the first time since I started to work in Nigeria I was invited to someone's home for lunch. Chima, the art director from the advertising agency and I had became great pals through the years. We shared a love for comics. Chima's wife prepared wonderful food and the two of us managed to finish off a bottle of Johnny Walker Black. Then we moved on to a bar a few blocks from the house.

It was time for a joint. In all my travels through Nigeria I had often heard of the legendary NNG, Nigerian Naturally Grown. It inspired Lil' Wayne to write a song about it and Snoop Doggy Dog asked for a takeaway. I wanted to put it to the test. Chima, quite willing after an afternoon's drinking in the sun, agreed to get me some.

When we drove off he didn't say where we were going. We stopped in an open veldt where a lot was still going on at midnight on a Sunday night. Over the veld dagga smoke hung as thick as Johannesburg's smog in winter. The joints didn't belong to anyone. Someone would roll one and when he got his fill it was passed on to the next person. I am allergic to caffeine, but I started drinking Red Bull to get me going again. I didn't want to miss a single second of the evening.

After puffing for half an hour Chima told me with a big smile that he had a surprise for me. We walked around the corner and the legendary The Shrine was right in front of me. At two o'clock that Monday morning I walked into a dancing mass of about 2 000 people. I was drunk on Johnny, high on NNG and wired on caffeine.

I only left the club at daybreak. I was struck by the new day and the fact that I had no idea of what lay ahead. One thing I did know and that was that a new life and many adventures waited. The future was so bright, I had to put on my shades.

# EPILOGUE

**T**HERE ARE SEVERAL theories about how the Maas clan ended up in Africa. One story goes that they were Scottish mercenaries who were prohibited from returning to their home country in the late 1600s after they participated in a war in what is today Germany. They were all given German surnames and in an effort to get rid of them, they were put on a boat destined for Cape Town.

Another, far more romantic version is that the ironsmith George Michael Maas fell in love with the daughter of his boss, a member of the Prussian nobility. To get away from the gossipmongers the two lovebirds had to flee to the Cape, most probably with her daddy's help.

It's not important which of these stories is true. Fact is, the Maas family has lived in Africa for quite some time, we speak a language that was created on this continent and we only have South African passports. I believe this makes me an African even though my skin is white.

Unfortunately, my whiteness seems to be a problem, because everywhere I travel in Africa I have to explain why I call myself an African. It isn't just accepted automatically. Some black Africans say that no white man can call himself African. Many of them even believe that a black American is more entitled to call himself African than a white South African whose family has been living on the continent for decades. The argument is that black Americans didn't have a choice about where they were taken to as slaves, but that the whites in Africa have always had the choice of whether to come here or not. This, of course, is a nonsensical argument.

So, are you entitled to call yourself a white African without sounding as if you are trying to make a political statement? I think so. There are literally thousands of tribes on our continent and the Afrikaner is but one of them. The Western media tend to portray our continent as being a homogenous, black mass with a few white spots in between. That is just as senseless as the theory about black Americans being African. There are as many differences and possible communication gaps between a Zulu and a Yoruba as there is between me and a Zulu, or me and a Yoruba.

I don't believe that I saw Rwanda, Nigeria and Madagascar through specifically white eyes. I think that I experienced those countries as an ordinary South African would. If a black South African were to take a similar trip he would experience the same absurdities. He would also have noticed the similarities and differences, have commented on the dissimilarity and have regaled his friends with stories around a braai.

Because I look at Africa as a fellow African, I'm allowed to focus my attention on all the good things that are happening on my continent, but also on what is wrong. I'm not an outsider who points out mistakes, but a local who is allowed to criticise, because I have been around long enough to do so. My idea certainly wasn't to ridicule Africa. This continent of ours is weird enough – you don't have to go out of your way to point it out.

Of course it's easier to see the mote in another's eye and not the beam in one's own. If I had to look at South Africa in the same way as I look at other African countries, I would notice many of the same absurdities (and wrongs). For instance, you only need to go to Bree Street's taxi rank to see a typical African delicacy: roughly cut pieces of meat that did not come from the abattoir and yes, it will be covered with flies. And when you walk in Brixton's streets, you'll also see graffiti on walls saying: "Do not urinate here."

According to police statistics 9 1 2 people died in police detention in South Africa in 2007/2008. However, according to Francois Beukman, Head of Investigations of the Independent Complaints Directorate, these figures do not indicate an increase in misconduct by the police. Or what about the Robben Island ferry that breaks down every so often. When it was out of action for five days last year there was no plan B and the loss in income was R1,7 million.

But it is also true that it is so easy to focus only on the negative in your own country and forget everything that is good about it. You often have to move around with and talk to tourists first before your eyes open up to its true splendour.

In the end I feel privileged that I, as member of a small tribe in Africa, could meet my fellow Africans on their home field and that so many of them trusted me enough to share their thoughts with me. Most of them welcomed and accepted me as African. If only the same could happen in my own country.

# SUGGESTED READING

**A few reasons to switch off the tv:**

*Africa Today*, Al J. Venter

*Congo Journey*, Redmond O'Hanlon

*Deogratias: a Tale of Rwanda*, J.P. Stassen

*Die Staf van Monomotapa*, Elsa Joubert

*Fela: From West Africa to West Broadway*, Trevor Schoonmaker (ed)

*I Live Here*, Mia Kirshner, J.B. Mackinnon, Paul Shoebridges, Michael Simons

*I Wouldn't Start from Here: The 21ˢᵗ Century and Where It All Went Wrong*, Andrew Mueller

*In the Footsteps of Mr Kurtz: Living on the Brink of Disaster in Mobutu's Congo*, Michaela Wong

*June 12: The Struggle for Power in Nigeria*, Abraham Oshoko

*King Leopold's Ghost: A Story of Greed, Terror and Heroism in Colonial Africa*, Adam Hochschild

*Kinshasa: Tales of the Invisible City*, Filip De Boeck & Marie-Françoise Plissart

*Lost Cosmonaut*, Daniel Kalder

*Music is the Weapon of the Future: Fifty Years of African Popular Music*, Frank Tenaille and Akwa Betote

*My Traitor's Heart*, Rian Malan

*Nzeogwu: An Intimate Portrait of Major Chukwuma Kaduna Nzeogwu*, Olusegun Obasanjo

*On The Road to Kandahar: Travels Through Conflict in the Islamic World*, Jason Burke

*Poisoned Wells: The Dirty Politics of African Oil*, Nicholas Shaxson

*Scribbling the Cat*, Alexandra Fuller

*Shake Hands with the Devil: The Failure of Humanity in Rwanda*, Lt Gen Roméo Dallaire

*The Hyena and Other Men*, Pieter Hugo

*The Ends of the Earth: From Togo to Turkmenistan, from Iran to Cambodia — A Journey to the Frontiers of Anarchy*, Robert D. Kaplan

*The Journey is the Destination: The Journals of Dan Eldon*, Dan Eldon and Kathy Eldon

*The Shadow of The Sun*, Ryszard Kapuściński

*The Unknown Soldier*, Joshua Dysart with sketches by Alberto Ponticelli

*The Wizard of the Nile: The Hunt for Africa's Most Wanted*, Matthew Green

*This House Has Fallen: Midnight in Nigeria*, Karl Maier

*Travels in West Africa*, Mary Kingsley

## When you're on the couch anyway: Documentaries

*General Idi Amin Dada: A self portrait* (1974)

*Africa Addio* (1966)

*Cry Freetown* (2000)

*Congo River, Beyond Darkness* (2005)

*As Old As My Tongue: The Myth and The Life of Bi Kidude* (2006)

*Johnny en die Maaiers* (2008)

*Konkombe: Nigerian Pop Music* (2000)
*Suffering and Smiling* (2006)
*Fela Kuti: Music is the Weapon* (2004)

## Websites

www.afropop.org

allafrica.com

awesometapesfromafrica.blogspot.com

combandrazor.blogspot.com

electricjive.blogspot.com

www.frootsmag.com

matsuli.blogspot.com

www.musicvideos.the-real-africa.com

www.vetseun.co.za

# ABOUT THE AUTHOR

**D**EON MAAS IS well known for having opinions that aren't necessarily shared by most people… But this doesn't deter him
in the least.

As a columnist for several Afrikaans newspapers, he has become
known for his outspoken and often controversial views on a range
of issues. Deon is a news junkie and a voracious reader with a keen
interest in African politics, travel and photography. He runs his own
media consultancy called Meerkat Media that's produced several do-
cumentaries, including *My Big Fat Afrikaner Wedding* and *Durban Poison*.

Deon is an ex-journalist, ex-television talkshow host, ex-record
company executive and ex-husband. He also dabbles in radio and
currently presents a radio show on South African protest music on
radio sonder grense (rsg).